T0340781

The Palestinian–Israeli Conflict: A Very Short Introduction

VERY SHORT INTRODUCTIONS are for anyone wanting a stimulating and accessible way in to a new subject. They are written by experts, and have been published in more than 45 languages worldwide.

The series began in 1995, and now represents a wide variety of topics in history, philosophy, religion, science, and the humanities. The VSI Library now contains more than 350 volumes—a Very Short Introduction to everything from ancient Egypt and Indian philosophy to conceptual art and cosmology—and will continue to grow in a variety of disciplines.

Very Short Introductions available now:

Available soon:

For more information visit our website
www.oup.com/vsi

Martin Bunton

THE PALESTINIAN– ISRAELI CONFLICT

A Very Short Introduction

OXFORD

UNIVERSITY PRESS

Great Clarendon Street, Oxford, ox2 6DP,
United Kingdom

Oxford University Press is a department of the University of Oxford.
It furthers the University's objective of excellence in research, scholarship,
and education by publishing worldwide. Oxford is a registered trade mark of
Oxford University Press in the UK and in certain other countries

© Martin Bunton 2013

The moral rights of the author have been asserted

First Edition published in 2013

Published in the United States of America by Oxford University Press
198 Madison Avenue, New York, NY 10016, United States of America

British Library Cataloguing in Publication Data
Data available

ISBN 978–0–19–960393–0

Printed and bound by CPI Group (UK) Ltd, Croydon, CR0 4YY

Contents

Acknowledgements

Many colleagues, students, friends, and family members have contributed to this book, and it is a pleasure to acknowledge them. I am deeply indebted to Gregory Blue, Christopher Ross, and Michael Thornhill who read carefully through numerous drafts, correcting mistakes and offering suggestions. Special thanks also to Avi Shlaim for his support and judicious advice and Mouin Rabbani for generously sharing his wisdom. Many academic colleagues and friends at the University of Victoria have stimulated my thinking in various ways, including Paul Bramadat, Rod Dobell, Andrew Rippin, Gus Thaiss, and Andew Wender. And it is very important that I acknowledge the influence—direct and indirect—of the many scholars of the Middle East whose published works have guided me, and I have tried to recognize this debt in both the References and Further reading sections at the end of the book. Only the author, of course, bears any responsibility for errors in fact or interpretation. I also wish to thank the numerous undergraduate students in the University of Victoria History Department, as well as local community groups and organizations, with whom I have attempted over two decades to share my knowledge, and questions. I especially thank Martin Hoffman, Ezra Karmel, and Christina Winter for their astute observations and research assistance.

I am most grateful to Emma Ma for her patience and support at all stages of the publishing process. At OUP, I also thank Luciana O'Flaherty, Kerstin Demata, Andrea Keegan, Carol Carnegie, Prabha Parthiban, Kevin Doherty, and Mike at Chartwell illustrations.

As always, my very special thanks go to Eila, Peter, and Seth (and, yes, Cleo). That this book has finally seen the light of day is primarily due to the constant encouragement and love of my wife Saija.

Preface

Over the last 120 years the evolving Palestinian–Israeli conflict has had many facets, but none has been as pressing and tangible as the problem of sharing the land. Too often, general weariness with the seemingly unending cycle of violence between Israelis and Palestinians has reinforced an ahistorical notion of the conflict as an ancient and religious one. By contrast, this *Very Short Introduction* reduces it to a modern territorial contest: two nations, one land. The main challenge to resolving the conflict is essentially one of drawing borders.

Accordingly, this book focuses squarely on the constant but evolving challenge of sharing a relatively small but geographically varied strip of land sitting between the Mediterranean Sea and the Jordan River. The six chapters of this book, organized chronologically, chart the failure of successive attempts to establish independent states that satisfy the claims of both Jewish and Palestinian nationalism to the same territorial space. Each section covers the span of a twenty-year (with the exception of one ten-year) period: 1897–1917; 1917–37; 1937–47; 1947–67; 1967–87; and 1987–2007. The chapters are organized around detailed examinations of pivotal historical junctions: the 1897 Basel Congress; the 1917 Balfour Declaration and British occupation of Palestine; the 1937 Peel partition plan and the violence of the Arab revolt; the 1947 United Nations (UN) partition plan and the outbreak of the war for Palestine; the 1967 war; and lastly, the 1987 *intifada*. At the risk of being overly linear, this approach ensures historical breadth. One of the main premises of this book is that there can be no assessment of the present, nor discussion of the future, without an understanding of how the conflict unfolded from the beginning. And by highlighting the many layers of complexity that have been added to the conflict over successive periods of time, focused attention on these bidecadal turning points also usefully reveals the cyclical nature of the conflict: these historical junctures gain much of their significance by the way they serve, somewhat paradoxically, as both spurs for potential resolution and motivations for further conflict—holding the promise to finally cut the Gordian knot of the territorial conflict, while at the same time tightening it.

In 1897, at the World Zionist Organization meeting held in Basel, Switzerland, Zionist leaders identified Palestine as the land in which to build a Jewish national home and secure for Jews their own state. In 1917, the Zionist movement was then provided the necessary catalyst when Palestine came under the foreign rule of a British government that during the First World War had allied itself to the Zionist cause. In Hebrew, the territory of Palestine was referred to as *Eretz Israel*, the land of Israel. But Zionism's geographic definition of a homeland has been problematic, pragmatic, and fluid. Facilitated by British rule over Palestine during the interwar period, Zionist settlement patterns focused strategically on Palestine's agriculturally rich valleys and coastal plains, largely disregarding the centres of ancient Jewish civilization that were located in Palestine's central hilly regions. This geographical division between the plains and the hills led to a profound redefinition of the territorial location of the Jewish homeland in the first half of the 20th century. When the 1937 Peel partition plan and the 1947 UN partition plan proposed a Jewish state be established in Palestine, they mapped out the coastal and valley areas, where Zionist land purchases were highest relative to the landholdings of the indigenous Arab population. Zionist leaders pragmatically built support for the idea of partition on strategic reasons, not religious ones: 'Erect a Jewish State at once,' wrote David Ben Gurion, 'even if it is not in the whole land.' Thus, when Zionist leaders celebrated in 1947 their most prominent diplomatic achievement—the two-thirds majority vote in the UN General Assembly in favour of partition—they accepted a state that included neither Jerusalem, which was meant to be internationalized, nor the hill lands of their forefathers (known in the Bible as Judea and Samaria) which were annexed by Jordan's King Abdullah and came to be known as the West Bank portion of his kingdom.

The boundaries established by the 1947 UN partition plan were rejected by the Palestinian Arabs. They viewed all of mandate Palestine as their national patrimony, a belief based on their long-standing presence as an overwhelming majority at the time of the 1917 British occupation. Denied the promise of self-determination following the First World War, when they constituted 90 per cent of the population, Palestinians found themselves under a British imperial administration whose commitment to Zionism was perceived as a grave threat to their national identity. Conflict was inevitable, and with every round of violence and negotiations Palestinian Arabs witnessed a gradual but marked recession of the actual portion of land available for the establishment of their state. The 1937 Peel partition plan envisaged an Arab state on approximately 75 per cent of mandate Palestine; the 1947 UN partition plan reduced that amount to 44 per cent; and, when armistice lines brought the subsequent fighting to a close in 1949, only 22 per cent was left outside the borders of the new state of Israel.

The 1947–49 war for Palestine created a refugee problem of immense proportions and, for the next few decades, Palestinians rejected any official recognition of the new state of Israel. But a new set of political equations was created by the 1967 war and the 1987 *intifada*. Israel finally came to be accepted by most

Palestinians as a permanent presence. Palestinians' support for a diplomatic compromise with Israel was driven by a commitment to having their own sovereign, independent country. In 1988, the Palestinian leadership officially accepted partition of what was mandate Palestine as offering the necessary chance for a peaceful resolution to their century-old conflict with Zionism. Acceptance of Israel on 78 per cent of mandate Palestine was put forth as a historic compromise. They claimed 100 per cent of the 22 per cent that remained.

Israel, however, viewed the Palestinian compromise as the start of negotiations, not an end. The reason for this was that, following Israel's 1967 conquest and occupation of the West Bank and Gaza, increasing numbers of Israelis demanded expanded control beyond Israel's borders. Now that they controlled the hilly lands steeped in Biblical antiquity, some Israelis argued a God-given right to establish a dominant Jewish presence there. The post-1967 growth of Jewish settlements in the Palestinian occupied territories was seen by the rest of the world as a contravention of international law (which prohibits the transfer of people from the occupying state to the occupied area). But in the battle for Israeli public support, the pro-settlement lobby described themselves as the present embodiment of the Zionist settlement movement: how, they asked, can Jewish rights to the Tomb of the Patriarchs in Hebron or Rachel's Tomb near Bethlehem, and other ancient sites located in the hills of the West Bank (what they referred to as Judea and Samaria), be less than to the plains and valleys which decades earlier defined the borders of the Zionist state? This profound struggle for the definition of Israeli society, and for the meaning and borders of a Jewish state, continues to this day, and in its outcome rests the future of Palestinians as well.

As the title suggests, the focus of this *Very Short Introduction* is the Palestinian–Israeli conflict. Of course, the conflict has from the start been at the centre of international attention and embroiled in the designs of foreign powers for strategic and economic influence. Up to this day, four key phases of international relations can be differentiated: the Ottoman, the European, the superpower, and the American. Of these, the period of European rule has been of paramount influence. Britain's rule over Palestine lasted only three decades, 1917–48. It was long enough, nonetheless, for both the establishment of a state government and, concurrently, the elaboration of ethno-religious fractures that would contribute to the state's eventual partition. Following the Second World War, the process of European decolonization, as was happening around the world, offered opportunities to the two new superpowers, the United States and the Soviet Union, to expand their influence. Renewed rounds of fighting between Israel and its Arab neighbours played a decisive role in embroiling the Middle East in the Cold War competition for global supremacy.

Equally, the conflict has been entangled in regional issues. Since 1937, various Arab regimes and ideological movements have offered their support to the Palestinian national cause. Though only a small proportion of the Arab peoples, the Palestinians have carried a disproportionate influence. Shibley Telhami has described the occupation and suffering of the Palestinian people as 'an open scar that is a reminder of a painful period in Arab history'. But it is important to note that the position of Palestinians in the Arab world has always been a complex one, caught between forces of cooperation and competition. To be sure, the ongoing conflict with Israel has offered useful opportunities for Arab regimes to bolster their own legitimacy by championing the Palestinian cause. But the festering resentment also played into the hands of militant Islamists and dissidents whose objectives were to overthrow those Arab regimes.

Wherever possible, close consideration will be given in this book to the significance of foreign intervention and regional trends. But the primary focus here is on the stubborn core of the conflict, the mutually exclusive territorial claims of two competing nationalisms, Palestinian and Israeli.

List of illustrations

The publisher and the author apologize for any errors or omissions in the above list. If contacted they will be happy to rectify these at the earliest opportunity.

Chapter 1
Ottoman Palestine 1897–1917

On 29 August 1897, Theodor Herzl convened the first Zionist Congress in the Swiss town of Basel. Over 200 delegates, most of whom had travelled from eastern Europe, gathered to discuss his nationalist plea for the creation of a new state in which Jews would form a majority of citizens. As a journalist working in Paris in the early 1890s, Herzl witnessed the appeal of anti-Semitism campaigns to French nationalist sentiments. This experience convinced him that even an assimilated Jew could never be accepted as an equal citizen in Europe. In 1896 he wrote *Der Judenstaat* (The Jewish State), setting out how the creation of a Jewish state would put an end to the prevailing anti-Semitism of Europe. The goal itself was not new. Earlier calls for a Jewish homeland had been made following the Russian pogroms of the early 1880s. The special achievement of Herzl's Basel programme was to establish the organizational structure necessary for the implementation of that goal. Delegates agreed to establish the World Zionist Organization as a permanent administration to direct the Zionist cause. They defined Zionism as 'the creation of a home for the Jewish people in Palestine'.

Palestine, however, was already inhabited. Many in Europe who hailed Zionism as a grand and noble project conceived of Palestine as empty. The Basel programme was launched at a time of great intellectual ferment, sparking bitter arguments among the leaders of Zionism about its secular nature, its dependence on the diplomatic support of imperial powers, and its relations to Jewish ancestral heritage in the land of Biblical Israel, referred to as *Eretz Israel*. But the delegates showed little interest in the goodwill of the Palestinian inhabitants, and it is this myopic thinking—'A land without a people for a people without a land' rang one prominent slogan—that lies at the heart of the Palestinian–Israeli conflict. Had Palestine in fact been empty, there would be no conflict as we know it. Some Jewish leaders did recognize this: Ahad Ha'am, for example, visited Palestine and observed that 'it is difficult to find fields that are not sowed'. He warned prophetically: 'If a time comes when our people in Palestine develop so that, in small or great measure, they push out the native inhabitants, these will not give up their place easily.'

This chapter examines the late 19th- and early 20th-century context in which two emerging national communities—Zionist and Palestinian—first collided over their mutually exclusive desire for the same piece of land, not much larger than Wales (approximately 16,000 square kms). Identifying 1897 as the beginning of the history of the Palestinian–Israeli conflict is significant. It underlines the fact that this hundred (or so) years' conflict is neither rooted in ancient and religious animosities nor even are its origins so much Middle Eastern as European. Just as European Jews were responding to the nationalist spirit spawned by the conditions in 19th-century Europe, so too was the identity of the indigenous Arab population about to be reshaped by the sharpening of a specifically Palestinian consciousness that formed around the inhabitants' resistance to the threat that Zionism posed to their own patrimony. It was in this context that Jewish immigrants from Europe struggled to find ways to successfully settle the land of Palestine, improvising and developing strategies that would have a huge impact on the future trajectory of the Zionist project.

'Political' versus 'labour' Zionism

While the 1897 Basel Congress may be commonly accepted as
marking the emergence of a coherent and political programme,
Zionism has never been a monolithic movement. Herzl's
conception of Zionism as primarily an international diplomatic, or
political, initiative met with opposition from a number of groups.
One challenge was posed by Jews who, in the decade prior to
the First World War, dispensed with diplomatic niceties and
emigrated to Palestine. Generally referred to as labour Zionists,
they advocated the importance of settlement work over
international diplomacy. A second important challenge would
emerge in the 1920s when Vladimir Jabotinsky founded the
Revisionist Party with the explicit goal of attaining statehood
by military force.

It is worth considering in some detail the divergent roles played by
the adherents of both political and labour Zionism. For Herzl's
part, his insistence that assimilation in Europe was impossible,
and that Jews could only be secure in a state of their own, was
motivated more by modern nationalist ideologies than by
traditional religious associations. His principal strategy was to
secure the political support of a great power and the financial
assistance of European Jewry. Indeed, he closely modelled his
plans along the lines of contemporaneous European colonizing
initiatives. A large-scale endeavour of overseas settlement such as
was envisaged by the Basel programme could never be successful,
Herzl argued, until it secured a 'charter' from a great power. He
devoted a great deal of his time to organizing audiences with
high-level government officials across Europe (including the
Russian Tsar and the Ottoman Sultan), but nothing substantial
came of his efforts. Notably, in 1903, his determination to find an
immediate refuge for Jews in danger of a new wave of pogroms led
Herzl to consider a British offer to colonize parts of East Africa.
This deal split the Zionist movement, alienating those Zionists
who sought settlement only in Palestine. The East African scheme

died with Herzl in 1904, following which the successful search for a powerful patron would have to wait for new diplomatic avenues forced opened by the First World War.

In the meantime, more practical figures set to work laying the foundations for a Zionist community on the land in Palestine. By 1914, approximately 85,000 Jews resided in Palestine, of whom about 35,000 had arrived in recent decades. This period of immigration consisted of two waves of settlement, known in Hebrew as *aliyot* (a single wave is an *aliyah*). The concept of *aliyah* (ascent) is fundamental to the Zionist principle that a Jewish state serve as a homeland for all the Jews in the world: emigration from Israel is referred to as *yerida* or 'descent'. Settlement conditions in Palestine were tenuous, and the first *aliyah* (1882–1903) encountered serious difficulties. Many settlers ended up leaving after a brief stay. Those communities that survived did so mainly due to their reliance on relatively cheap Arab labour and to the philanthropy of wealthy European Jews. In contrast, the more significant second *aliyah* (1904–14) gradually became more committed to the creation in Palestine of a separate society built on Jewish labour. These two groups tended to clash.

The main problem faced by the labour Zionists of the second *aliyah* was how to establish farming enterprises that were sufficiently viable to support a standard of living high enough to induce a continual flow of immigrants from eastern Europe. The second *aliyah*'s response took time to work out but the solutions eventually arrived at were critical in laying the foundations of the Jewish state four decades later. In his book *Land, Labor and the Origins of the Israeli–Palestinian Conflict, 1882–1914*, Gershon Shafir describes how, on the one hand, competition with lower-paid native workers and, on the other, the goal of finding jobs for Jewish immigrants led the leaders of the second *aliyah* to try to separate the Arab and Jewish societies and economies. From this strategy evolved the *kibbutz* movement, a programme of settlement based on cooperation among Jewish immigrants.

Generally referred to as 'the conquest of labour', the replacement of Arab workers by Jews was also justified by the need to form a new common Jewish identity linked to the soil. In the Zionist nationalist ethos, reclaiming the land was a way of rejecting the experience of life in the diaspora. The 'conquest of labour' was closely accompanied by the idea of a 'conquest of land'. In order to acquire—or, to use the quasi-religious terminology employed at the time, 'redeem'—the land of Palestine, the fifth Zionist Congress, held in Basel in 1901, set up the Jewish National Fund (JNF). Shafir quotes Menachem Ussishkin, president of the JNF and a major force behind Jewish land acquisitions:

> In order to establish autonomous Jewish community life—or, to be more precise, a Jewish state, in Eretz Israel, it is necessary, first of all, that all, or at least most, of Eretz Israel's lands will be the property of the Jewish people. Without ownership of the land, Eretz Israel will never become Jewish, be the number of Jews whatever it may be in the towns and even in the villages, and Jews will remain in the very same abnormal situation which characterizes them in the diaspora.

The JNF negotiated the purchase of Arab landholdings that would henceforth be regarded as inalienably Jewish. The scope of land purchase remained limited (in part due to restrictions implemented by the Ottoman government), and the agrarian ideal failed to be reflected in the emerging reality of a mostly urban Jewish population (by 1944, less than 25 per cent of the population was rural). Nonetheless, these efforts did shape the future of the Zionist project. The necessity of buying land was never a source of contention among the settlers; the more fundamental question was where to find it, and the answer would be found more in land that held economic promise than religious significance. Zionism's need to buy agricultural land had the singular importance of defining, or redefining, for Zionism the geographical location of Zion.

Most notably, the areas of Biblical significance known as Judea and Samaria, located more prominently in Palestine's mountainous areas, were shunned for the coastal plains and valleys. Part of the reason for this may have been a lack of religious interest: for example, David Ben Gurion, a leader of the second *aliyah*, centred labour Zionism's political and economic activities in Tel Aviv (he evidently did not visit Jerusalem until three years after his arrival). Some early Zionists adopted an agricultural identity as tillers of the soil as part of consciously turning their back on the diaspora. The bigger reason for purchasing land in the plains and valleys was the legal and economic opportunities that the landscape there offered. And to explore the implications of this further we need to turn our attention to Ottoman Palestine, and the changing political and social contexts in which labour Zionists sought to carve out their self-sufficient settlements.

Ottoman Palestine

For a relatively small and narrow territory, the land of Palestine contains a remarkable variety of soils, climates, and terrains. A glance at a relief map, as shown in Illustrations 1 and 2, shows the country falling topographically into two main divisions: the central mountainous range, running from south to north, and the coastal plains and inland valleys (with the remainder consisting of wide expanses of desert in the south). At the turn of the century, with Palestinian agriculture lacking sophisticated agricultural technology, it was these geographical features that largely determined agricultural conditions. The rich coastal plains and northern inland valleys possessed the important advantages of good soil, sufficient annual rainfall, and convenient transportation. Naturally, better agricultural possibilities were found there.

Farming in the plains and valleys produced a variety of products hungrily consumed in Europe—wheat, barley, and maize, for example—but the choice export item in Palestine was the juicy, thick-skinned, and easy to transport Jaffa orange. Citrus fruits

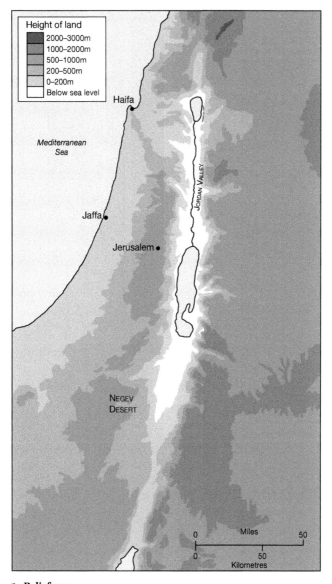

1. **Relief map**

The Palestinian–Israeli Conflict

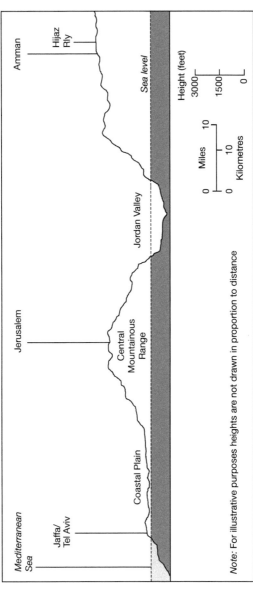

Note: For illustrative purposes heights are not drawn in proportion to distance

2. Relief cross section

were in high demand in European markets at the turn of the century, and the high profits justified the investment in irrigation and the time it took for young seedlings to bear fruit. The introduction of the internal combustion engine in 1897 allowed orchard owners to improve vastly their access to underground aquifers. Citrus acreage expanded significantly.

Nonetheless, the relative weakness of central Ottoman state power and policing at the beginning of the 19th century resulted in most of Palestine's rural population living in the safer mountainous terrain. The need for water and cultivable land had to be balanced against the more pressing need to protect oneself against attack, for example from Bedouin raids. Such considerations were of enormous importance during the early 19th century when Ottoman authorities were unable to provide the basic infrastructure required by agriculturalists interested in increasing their input of labour or capital. Accordingly, patterns of cultivation were determined more by the variable degree of security for the settled population than by geographic and climatic factors. Though some cultivation did continue in parts of the plains adjacent to the central mountainous range, through satellite villages known as *khirbehs*, generally Palestine witnessed a decline in the cultivated area during this period.

Areas that lay beyond the effective control of the Ottoman government at this time were dominated by competing local notable families, each with their own independent power base. The Ottomans could not have exercised effective authority without the notables' services, such as tax collecting. In return, the notables required access to government in order to fulfil the expectations of their followers. While notable politics was characterized by a degree of factional squabbling, notables remained active intermediaries for the Ottoman government.

These relationships underwent a major change in the mid 19th century, the effect of which was to push a western migration of the Palestinian population from the mountains into the valleys and plains. The context for this transformation was provided first by the results of the intense administrative reforms undertaken by the Ottoman government, known as the *Tanzimat*; and, secondly by the incorporation of the Ottoman Empire into the growing world economy.

The *Tanzimat* (literally 'reorganization') represented a great push by the Ottoman leadership to extend its governing apparatus throughout the empire. The adoption of new legal and administrative codes, often inspired by European bureaucracies, was designed to empower the central government in Istanbul. A key measure in this respect was the Ottoman land law of 1858. By requiring that all individuals who possessed land be provided with a title deed, the law aimed to establish a one-to-one relationship between the peasant cultivator and the state. The Ottoman government stood to benefit financially, by the efficient taxation of agricultural production, and administratively, by extending the authority of trained officials. The intent may also have been to undermine the position of the notables, but in fact they were the best positioned to take advantage of the regulations. Quick to appreciate the new opportunities to purchase and register lands, and attracted by the improved security conditions, notable families acquired vast tracts of land in the relatively more sparsely populated plains and valleys of Palestine. One particularly significant illustration (the fallout from which will be considered in the next chapter) of the overall trend was the purchase by the Sursuq family of about 50,000 acres in the plain of Esdraelon (also known as the Jezreel valley or, in Arabic, *Marj ibn Amr*).

The second important factor that contributed at this time to the growing interest in the agricultural potential of the plains and valleys was Palestine's increased connectedness—by railroads, shipping lines, a telegraph network—to the world economy. Europe's insatiable demand for raw materials resulted in a considerable increase in Palestine's agricultural output. This is revealed by the estimates available for the trade out of the port of Jaffa during this period: for example, while orange exports to the United Kingdom increased more than sixfold between 1860 and 1881, the export of cereals doubled between 1873 and 1881.

Market opportunities resulting from greater integration into the world market and the increased security of administrative reforms in the last part of the 19th century created increased pressure on the land and resources of Palestine's coastal plains and inland valleys. Settlement took a number of forms: Bedouin groups began to settle in permanent locales; satellite *khirbehs* were more densely and continuously inhabited as the more densely inhabited Arab villages in the mountainous areas repopulated the fertile plains; and rich notables were quick to invest in economic opportunities as they arose. And then, following the Russian pogroms of the early 1880s, European Jews started arriving. They too sought agricultural opportunities, sometimes backed up by the financial support of wealthy patrons. By the beginning of the 20th century, Zionism had established a dozen settlements on land that was usually bought from Arab notables who had themselves acquired legal ownership of the land within the last few decades, attracted by the profits to be made. Such legal and economic opportunities for land purchase did not exist in the mountainous areas of greatest significance to Biblical antiquity. Recognizing how early Zionist settlers avoided attributing special importance to religious sites, and instead took root in the fertile lands of the plains, explains why ultimately the boundaries of Israel—when they were defined and redefined in the diplomacy of 1947 and the fighting of 1948—did not in the end include the Biblical areas of Judea and Samaria. Control over that territory would only come after another twenty years.

Conclusion

Over the course of the 19th century, the structure of the Ottoman state was subject to an intense, if piecemeal, reform process. These reforms aimed at strengthening the central administration of the empire. Some Arab citizens, understandably enough, contested government attempts to increase its control over their society, but few actually challenged the sovereignty of the Ottoman state or gave much thought to a world without it. As Ottoman citizens, Arabs were given some representation in the parliament, participated in the expanding bureaucracy and enrolled in the growing school system. And it was the Ottoman army that ostensibly provided protection against the intervention of European powers, their missionaries, and their intermediaries.

Ultimately, this chapter's use of the term 'Palestine', while helpful in demarcating a well known geographical region, is anachronistic in reference to a political unit. Before the First World War, there was no 'Palestine' as such; rather the territory, as shown in Illustration 3, consisted of the districts of Jerusalem, Nablus, and Acre, all of which were defined according to an evolving framework of Ottoman administration. This has contributed throughout the 20th century to some political leaders contesting the existence of Palestinians. In 1969 Israeli Prime Minister Golda Meir famously remarked that there was no such thing: 'When was there an independent Palestinian people with a Palestinian state?…It was not as though there was a Palestinian people considering itself as Palestinian people and we came and threw them out and took their country away from them. They did not exist.' More recently, such sentiments were echoed by US Republican presidential hopeful Newt Gingrich: 'Palestinians are an invented people,' he declared. 'Remember, there was no Palestine as a state. It was part of the Ottoman Empire…And they had the chance to go many places.'

While it is true that Palestinian national identity would not arise until the British invasion and occupation of Ottoman land, and only consolidated itself as a result of the desire to both throw off the yoke of British imperial rule and resist Zionist immigration and settlement, the more important point to note is that all

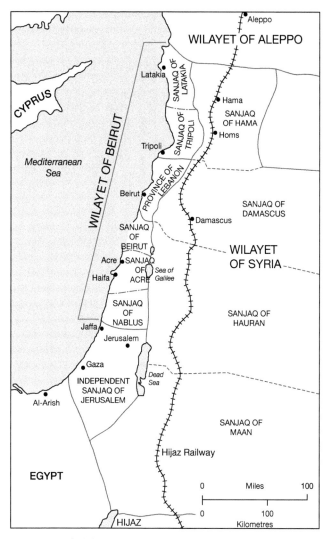

Ottoman Palestine 1897–1917

3. **Ottoman administrative divisions**

nationalisms arise and gather strength from specific historical circumstances. This includes Zionism, as constructed by the small but fractious minority of Jews who chose it as their national identity. As a national movement, Zionism rose to prominence in the late 19th century in opposition to the consistent persecution of Jews by newly emergent nationalist movements across Europe. This does not make it any less invented, or any more valid, than other nationalisms. When European Zionist leaders struck out to consolidate their position on the ground in Palestine, they were forced to respond to the presence of the indigenous Arab society and to the geography in which its economy was developing. The most remarkable component of this evolution was the territorial shift in the geographical definition of the land of Zion.

Significant as this shift would become, the overall achievement was still quite limited. When Herzl returned to Vienna following the 1897 Basel Congress, he reflected happily on its achievements by writing in his diary that 'in Basel I created the Jewish State' and that 'five years hence, in any case, certainly fifty years hence, everyone will perceive it'. Accurate though Herzl's statement appears in hindsight, one must nonetheless take great care not to read history backwards. In fact, the triumphalist hopes of Zionist leaders in 1897 were soon enough dashed by the actual failure to achieve any real objective. Of the 2.5 million Russian Jews who emigrated between 1882 and 1914, less than 50,000 made their way to the dreamed-of Jewish homeland in Palestine. And many of them did not stay for long. Those who did were able to acquire ownership of only a tiny percentage of the land. Herzl was right that Zionism needed a major diplomatic breakthrough. But that would have to wait twenty years, when the First World War presented the unique opportunity.

Chapter 2
British Palestine 1917–37

The First World War (1914–18) has been described as the most transformative event in the history of the modern Middle East. The British army's occupation of Arab territories ended four centuries of Ottoman rule over them. An entirely new political map emerged as six new successor states from the former Ottoman Empire were created: Turkey, Lebanon, Syria, Iraq, Palestine, and Transjordan. In Anatolia, former Ottoman military commanders were able to rally to secure the national independence of Turkey. But in the five new Arab states the post-war period was one of Anglo-French dominance. European rule was sanctioned by the newly formed League of Nations through the mandate system, an institution that tried to gloss over the fact that colonial relationships were being imposed on the ground despite US President Woodrow Wilson's proposals for self-determination.

This chapter sets out the ways in which Britain carved out and then ruled over the newly created state of Palestine—a quixotic, and ultimately doomed, experiment in facilitating Arab-Zionist cohabitation in a single state. Britain's rule over Palestine lasted only three decades. It was long enough, nonetheless, for both the establishment of new national frameworks (a capital city, for example, as well as a new currency and trade agreements along newly defined borders) and, concurrently, the elaboration of ethno-religious fractures that would contribute to Palestine's eventual partition. A complex tangle of constitutional, immigration, and land ownership issues, Britain's failed attempts up to 1937 to reconcile the mutually exclusive demands for self-determination among Palestine's Arab and Jewish communities, led inevitably to the intensifying conflict between them. The Arab–Jewish fault line would then be fundamentally transformed in the 1937–47 period by a unique clash of converging forces.

The promised land?

Britain's long-standing strategic concern in the eastern Mediterranean was to protect the overland trade route to India and, after its opening in 1869, the Suez Canal, which quickly came to be regarded as the jugular vein of Empire. Beyond that, the main aim of British diplomacy prior to the First World War was to preserve the territorial integrity of the Ottoman Empire so as to guard against Russian expansionism. When the Ottomans allied with Germany, British leaders were forced to rethink how best to protect their interests in the Middle East. They were willing to consider multiple conflicting plans, all in the hope of securing a military victory.

By the time the war ended, Britain had put her signature on a confusing array of promises and declarations. She had pledged the future disposition of Palestine to no less than three different real or imagined allies. First, Britain's high commissioner in Egypt, Sir Henry McMahon, made promises to Sharif Husayn, the Hashemite ruler of the Hijaz region of Arabia, about the creation of an independent Arab kingdom. Secondly, Britain officially recognized the long-standing claims of her French allies to Syria, while staking claims of her own. Third, promises were made to Zionist leaders in London. A fourth set of commitments, spurred by US President Woodrow Wilson, was broadcast about the rights of all peoples to independence and self-determination. The end result was a complex tangle of pledges and counter-pledges. British diplomats would do their best in the post-war years to square the contradictions, but these wartime agreements have remained to this day the source of much controversy and resentment.

By the terms of the first negotiations—worked out during an exchange of letters between July 1915 and March 1916 commonly referred to as the Husayn–McMahon correspondence—Britain pursued an anti-Ottoman alliance with Sharif Husayn. As protector of Mecca and Medina, Islam's holiest cities, Husayn oversaw the annual pilgrimage. A leader of such religious authority could, Britain hoped, reverse the call to *jihad* issued by the Ottoman sultan-caliph to stir up trouble among Muslims in the British Empire, particularly India. Better yet, perhaps Husayn, who before the war had been feeling increasingly threatened by Istanbul's efforts to assert closer control over the Hijaz, would rise against Ottoman forces and take some pressure off Britain's position at the Suez Canal.

In return for a Hashemite-led revolt, Britain promised to recognize Sharif Husayn as ruler of an independent Arab kingdom. Much ambiguity surrounded the status of such a realm, not least the demarcation of its territorial boundaries. The place of Palestine in the assurances made by Britain became the subject of fierce debate when Britain was forced to defend its divisive policies in Palestine by interpreting the correspondence in a way that specifically excluded it from any prior promises made to Arabs. Its failure to argue this position successfully made British imperial rule across the Middle East all the more resented: 'a startling piece of double-dealing,' wrote George Antonius, a Palestinian leader and one of the first historians of Arab nationalism. British obfuscation, born out of wartime desperation, is perhaps best captured by Sir Henry McMahon's own explanation for the inherent ambiguity of his assurances: 'What we have to arrive at now is to tempt the Arab people into the right path, detach them from the enemy and bring them on to our side. This on our part is at present largely a matter of words, and to succeed we must use persuasive terms and abstain from academic haggling over conditions.'

At the same time as negotiating with Sharif Husayn, British officials were meeting with their European counterparts in order to divvy up the Middle East as the potential spoils of the still unfinished war. The second controversial set of promises, known as the 1916 Sykes–Picot Agreement, recognized French claims to the northern parts of the Arab territories (the future Lebanon and Syria), while guaranteeing British interests and influence in the southern part (from Egypt to Iraq). Both Britain and France wanted Palestine. In the end the agreement placed it under the control of an 'international administration', the precise definition of the term being left for the future, while giving Britain the ports of Haifa and Acre.

Over the next year, however, Britain recalculated its own strategic interests in the future status of Palestine. The region was the site of important military operations, and government officials concluded that Palestine's value as a buffer to the Suez Canal had become too important to allow for an ill-defined international presence there after the war. These new interests were being defined just as British forces were amassing in the Sinai Peninsula to push back the Ottoman forces and break through to Palestine. Moreover, these new calculations developed in tandem with the efforts of the leading members of Britain's Jewish community who, in pursuit of the strategies of political Zionism, sought to persuade the government that Zionist interests complemented British interests. Accordingly, in November 1917, in a letter addressed by Arthur James Balfour, the British Secretary of State for Foreign Affairs, to Lord Walter Rothschild, a prominent member of the British Jewish community, Britain announced that 'His Majesty's Government view with favour the establishment in Palestine of a national home for the Jewish people.' Of the three sets of commitments Britain made over this much-promised land, the Balfour Declaration would be the most enduring.

Foreign Office

2nd November 1917

Dear Lord Rothschild,

I have much pleasure in conveying to you, on behalf of His Majesty's Government, the following declaration of sympathy with Jewish Zionist aspirations which has been submitted to, and approved by, the Cabinet:

'His Majesty's Government view with favour the establishment in Palestine of a national home for the Jewish people, and will use their best endeavours to facilitate the achievement of this object, it being clearly understood that nothing shall be done which may prejudice the civil and religious rights of existing non-Jewish communities in Palestine, or the rights and political status enjoyed by Jews in any other country.'

I should be grateful if you would bring this declaration to the knowledge of the Zionist Federation.

Yours sincerely,

Arthur James Balfour

The history and purpose of the Balfour Declaration remain controversial subjects. At heart, the aligning of British interests with those of Zionism was underpinned by two racialized beliefs. One was the conception that Jews constituted a nation. A second fundamental precept of British policy was that Palestine's Arab inhabitants themselves did not merit attention beyond an idealized consideration of the improvements European colonization brought to backward areas. These cultural preconceptions are boldly captured in Lord Balfour's own famous justification of his declaration: 'Zionism, be it right or wrong, good or bad,' he wrote in 1922, was 'rooted in age-long traditions, in present needs and future hopes of far profounder import than the desires and prejudices of the 700,000 Arabs who now inhabit that ancient land.'

In addition to wartime strategic interests, a complex combination of motives led to the final decision to issue the Balfour Declaration. Contemporary explanations tended to stress the Biblical romanticism of British officials' interest in the restoration of the Jewish nation in Palestine and their sympathy for the plight of Jews in eastern Europe. The first scholarly accounts focused more on the political and diplomatic context in which British officials came to see Zionism as an ally. These early interpretations stressed the Balfour Declaration as a product of the activities of the Zionist Organization, or specifically of Dr Chaim Weizmann, the most prominent Zionist spokesman. Weizmann was engaged during the war in biochemical research for Britain's Ministry of Munitions. His influential contacts and skilful persistence were credited with convincing British officials of the wartime propaganda value that a gesture of support for Zionism would carry in the United States and Russia, where Jews were believed to wield great power.

As government sources became more widely available, historians shifted the focus away from Zionist leaders and instead laid more stress on the actions of those British officials who in fact searched out Zionist support in pursuit of their own interests in Palestine. Their main aim was to keep the French out. Within a year of having negotiated the terms of the 1916 Sykes–Picot Agreement which called for the international administration of Palestine, Britain came round to fearing any foreign presence so close to the Suez Canal. As Mayir Vereté conjectured: 'had there been no Zionists in those days the British would have had to invent them'.

Historians in recent years have again shifted their attention. From an emphasis on the presumed rationales that motivated the decision-making process, they have begun to analyse more fully the prejudices that belied British support for Zionism. These studies argue that, in order for British officials to even consider using Zionism in any sort of strategic way, they had to draw upon a reserve of mistaken, even anti-Semitic, ideas and of a homogenized Jewish 'nation', all of which tended to greatly exaggerate the power and influence of world Jewry. Such notions ignored the multitude of identities that constituted modern Jewish politics in which, as was discussed in the first chapter, Zionists were only a small minority.

In the month following Balfour's declaration, British forces occupied Jerusalem. Now in charge of large parts of Palestine, British authorities on the ground tried to tone down the effect of their government's pro-Zionist policy. Much to the chagrin of the Zionist leadership, no practical initiatives were allowed by the military administration as it tried to restore order and stability to a war-torn landscape. But as word of the Balfour Declaration made its way to Palestine, its Arab population became increasingly wary of the evident challenge Zionism posed. In November 1918, on the first anniversary of the Balfour Declaration, which coincided with the final end to the war and an opening up of political activity, Arab dignitaries and representatives petitioned the British, denouncing the Balfour Day parade that was held in Jerusalem. From this point on, Zionism became the chief factor in the articulation of a Palestinian Arab nationalist identity.

But the hostility directed towards Zionism in Palestine did not deter the British government in London, which maintained its support for Zionism. This was especially important when, at the 1920 San Remo conference, the Supreme Allied Council awarded Britain the 'mandate' for Palestine. The genesis of the mandate idea lies in the tension that emerged between the Allies' desire for the spoils of war, and President Wilson's call for an end to the secret diplomacy of European empires. The wartime slogan most closely associated with President Wilson, 'the war to make the world safe for democracy', both greatly bolstered the Allied war effort, by endowing it with a noble rationale, and gravely threatened the Allied war aims in the region, which focused on expansion of European rule into the Arab lands of the former Ottoman Empire.

Britain's status as mandatory ruler for Palestine was officially recognized in 1923 by the newly formed Council of the League of Nations. The League demarcated different classes of mandates. Whereas for 'B' and 'C' mandates longer periods of trusteeship were proposed, 'A' mandates constituted countries judged by the council to have already 'reached a stage of development where their existence as independent nations can be provisionally recognized subject to the rendering of administrative advice and assistance by a Mandatory until such time as they are able to stand alone'. The Arab lands of the former Ottoman Empire, including Palestine, were all defined as 'A' mandates. In many ways, the invention of the mandate system was the means by which Britain and France also disguised old-fashioned imperial acquisition as enlightened tutelage. Nonetheless, by accepting the mandate system, Britain and France officially accepted responsibility for preparing these new states for self-determination, even as they were at the same time trying to protect their own strategic interests.

A tricky balancing act throughout the region, the mandate system was especially problematic in Palestine, the mandate for which incorporated the entire text of the Balfour Declaration, thus placing the small Jewish minority, composing about 10 per cent of the population, in a uniquely privileged position. The mandate also included several articles specifying the obligation of Britain, as mandatory power, to support the establishment of a Jewish national home in Palestine (for example, facilitating Jewish immigration and encouraging Jewish settlement on the land). Meanwhile, as was the case with the Balfour Declaration itself, not once was the Palestinian Arab population mentioned by name. Once the Balfour Declaration was written into the terms of the mandate that sanctioned British rule in Palestine, one of several competing wartime promises was turned into a more binding contract mediated by the League of Nations. As the British administration in Palestine came to feel the pressure of being caught in the escalating conflict between the mutually exclusive nationalist demands of the Jewish and the Arab communities, many officials wanted to reconsider the promise of imposing a Jewish national home on an Arab majority. However, Britain also felt the constraints imposed by the internationally monitored mandate document and found it highly problematic to rescind the promise.

British administration

Though Palestine was recognized as an 'A' mandate, Britain effectively ran it as a 'Crown colony' for its first two decades (see Illustration 4). In Jerusalem, governing power was limited to the appointed high commissioner and his own council of British officials (mostly ex-officers who had arrived as part of the military operations of the First World War). Meanwhile, in London control passed in 1921 from the Foreign Office to the Colonial Office, where officials of a Middle East department assisted the Secretary of State for the Colonies in managing affairs, all of whom operated under the watchful eye of the British Treasury. London's prominent place in the policy-making process meant that British rule in Palestine was frequently subject to the mediation and pressure exercised by external political parties and groups.

The deliberate ambiguity of the term 'Jewish national home' as raised in the Balfour Declaration meant that nobody really knew what in fact London had in mind for Palestine. Zionist leaders, for their part, were clear that a national home meant a Jewish state and expected the British to accept this to be the mandate's raison d'être. But the British had not committed themselves to such an interpretation, and failed at first to give much thought to precisely when they might regard a 'home' as being established. It seemed that Britain envisaged the establishment of a unitary Arab-Jewish

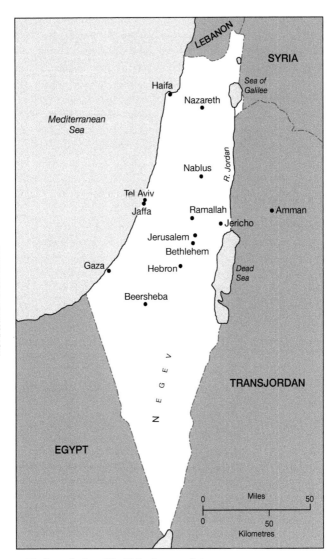

4. The boundaries of the Palestine mandate

state. In theory, this policy was seen as resulting from a 'dual obligation'. If only implicitly, it recognized the potential for intercommunal conflict. But it was common imperial practice to manipulate often-conflicting religious, ethnic, and other groups to maintain British interests.

What was unique in Palestine was the general failure to draw its cohabiting populations into basic mechanisms of government, such as a legislative assembly. Negotiations over some type of representative council were continually tripped up by the Palestinian Arab demand for power to control Zionist immigration and land purchase. This was something that the British were unprepared to concede. Britain demanded Arab acceptance of the terms of the mandate. Arabs feared that participation on such terms would be seen as tacit acknowledgement of the legitimacy of the Balfour Declaration. The only Middle Eastern colony to be denied a legislative council, Palestine was also, interestingly enough, the only newly crafted state in the region not to survive British decolonization intact. The failure to create a legislative council in Palestine represents a key turning point in the country's history. As D. K. Fieldhouse has observed, 'Seen in the larger context of British imperial history, legislative councils had been a crucial means of transferring power from the executive to representatives of the colonial population, even if the transition from official to non-official majority, and then to a government responsible to a legislature, was in most cases slow.'

For the first two decades of British rule, the power structures among the Arab population in Palestine remained dominated by traditional patron–client networks of local notables. Notables willingly acted as intermediaries with the British authorities as they had with the Ottomans. Meanwhile, leaders in neighbouring Arab states were increasingly accorded the powers of a national government, the potential sovereignty of which was never in doubt. Iraq, for example, gained formal independence in 1932, while in Egypt the consuming desire for independence was partially fulfilled in 1936.

The *Yishuv*

In contrast to the absence of any formally recognized body of Arab representatives, the mandate specifically enjoined Britain to establish a Jewish Agency for the purpose of empowering it with governmental institutions. Through the development of its own organizations in Palestine, the Jewish community (known as the *Yishuv*) constructed a European-style economy and society increasingly distinct from the indigenous Arab community. At the beginning of the mandate there were approximately 70,000 Jews out of a total settled population of over 700,000 inhabitants. Accordingly, large-scale Jewish immigration was considered crucial to achieve a significant demographic constituency. Zionism now benefited from British assistance, but Palestine still faced difficulty attracting large numbers. The actual number of immigrants at first disappointed, and at times embarrassed, Zionist leaders. By the end of the first decade, only 100,000 chose to immigrate to Palestine (in fact, from 1927 to 1928 Jewish emigration exceeded immigration). By contrast, between 1933 and 1936 approximately 170,000 Jews fled European anti-Semitism, especially in Germany and Poland. Known as the fifth *aliyah*, this wave of immigration effectively doubled the number of Jews living in Palestine, raising it to 30 per cent of the population. This fifth *aliyah* gave the *Yishuv* the numbers necessary to fulfil the Zionist dream. Composed of a higher number of professionals than earlier waves of immigrants, this *aliyah* also tended to prefer the coastal cities to the central hills.

The Jewish community in Palestine remained throughout the mandate a largely urban one. The acquisition of agricultural land on which to found rural settlements continued nonetheless to be a major focus of Zionist efforts. The image of the autonomous farming collective became a powerful symbol though less than

15 per cent of the *Yishuv* worked in agriculture. During the 1920s, Jewish landholdings nearly doubled, from 162,000 acres to almost 300,000. By the end of the mandate in 1947 another 175,000 acres were purchased, resulting in approximately 7 per cent of Palestine being acquired by Jewish land purchasing agencies. Though limited in scope, the transfer of land from Arab to Jewish ownership nevertheless had a demoralizing effect on the Palestinian Arab national movement. Together with 'the conquest of land', 'the conquest of labour' continued to be a central feature of Zionist activity in Palestine: land purchased by the Jewish National Fund (JNF) was leased exclusively to Jews. British officials never properly counted the number of Arab peasants evicted from their lands, but given the limited agricultural potential of the country, control over land became a focus of Palestinian nationalist activism in the 1930s.

The significance of these land purchases lies also, as will be recalled from the previous chapter, in their location: the fertile lands along the coast and in the inland valleys. This was where the best opportunities lay for Jewish land purchasing agencies. The high prices offered for land appealed especially to absentee Arab owners, such as the Sursuq family of Beirut, who had expanded their landholdings in the late 19th century but now found themselves on the wrong side of a new international border. Understandably, Arab notables were keen to make a profit on their late 19th-century investments in land. Jewish land purchases in the valleys and plains, as shown in Illustration 5, left an indelible stamp on the future of Palestine by the fact that they are so closely reflected in the shape given to Palestine's partition in 1947.

In addition to the JNF, several other organizations aimed at building the self-sufficiency of the *Yishuv*. The Jewish community in Palestine had its own taxation system, managed its own health care and education, and revived modern Hebrew as a living language (replacing Yiddish as the native language of most East

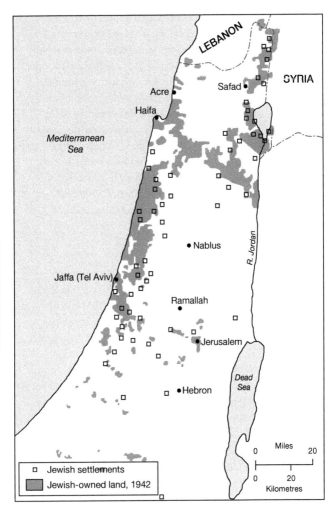

5. Jewish land purchases

European immigrants). One of the most important institutions of the *Yishuv* was *Histadrut*, the Federation of Jewish Labour. At first, its main role was to promote the employment of Jewish labour in Jewish enterprises, and to this end it instituted a boycott that targeted Arab workers. It continually expanded its activities until, by the end of the mandate, it was second only to the Palestine government as an employer of labour. *Histadrut* also took over more and more responsibility for defence, with its own military force known as *Haganah*. Though this force was illegal, the British rulers of Palestine lacked the will or capacity to do anything about it.

At the head of *Histadrut*, David Ben Gurion's Mapai party wielded a great deal of influence. Chaim Weizmann continued to play a significant role in influencing British policy-making, but not all Zionist groups adhered to his strategy of working within Britain's security umbrella to build an independent state. Of the various political organizations that competed with Ben Gurion's labour Zionism, three stand out. From one side of the spectrum, labour Zionism was contested by ultra-orthodox Jews who argued that Zionism itself was a heresy; from another, it was challenged from bi-nationalists, such as Judah Magnes, who campaigned for a more equal distribution of power in Palestine between Arabs and Jews. The most militant opposition came from Vladimir Jabotinsky, who in 1925 founded Revisionist Zionism. Jabotinsky challenged both Ben Gurion's socialist ideologies and Weizmann's more cautious reliance on Britain. He founded his own underground militia, the *Irgun Zvei Leumi* (generally referred to by its Hebrew acronym *Etzel*, but known to the British as Irgun) and called for Britain's immediate withdrawal and the proclamation of a Jewish commonwealth in both Palestine and Transjordan. Revisionists were particularly upset about the way in which borders had been established, arguing that in 1921 Transjordan was unfairly sliced off Palestine. This charge would develop into a powerful political myth, however baseless in fact. Before mandatory rule, there had, of course, been no formal state of Palestine from which the lands of Transjordan could have been severed. (As Bernard Wasserstein observes, it is more appropriate to view Transjordan as being added to the mandatory governance of Palestine than as severed from it.)

The Palestinian Arab community

In contrast to the structured and well connected Jewish leadership, the Palestinian Arab leadership suffered from paralysing divisions. While the Jewish Agency was left to build up its own para-state structures, the British played upon Arab rivalries by following well honed strategies of divide and rule that had successfully structured collaborative relationships with indigenous peoples in other colonial administrations. The building of these collaborative relationships was facilitated in Palestine by the desire of notable families who, having solidified their position in the late 19th century thanks to Ottoman policies such as the 1858 land law, were eager to secure their interests in the post-war period by continuing to act as intermediaries. Thus, the notables faced the daunting challenge of having to work within the mandate system at the same time as opposing the Zionist goals to which that system was bound.

One of the most influential families in Jerusalem was the Husayni family. They competed for power with the Nashashibi family. Playing on these divisions in particular, the British appointed Raghib bey al-Nashashibi mayor of Jerusalem in 1920 (replacing an al-Husayni) and then the following year selected Hajj Amin al-Husayni as Grand Mufti of Jerusalem. The authority of the position of Mufti of Jerusalem was greatly expanded in 1922 when Hajj Amin was elected to head a newly created institution called the Supreme Muslim Council (SMC). The SMC was responsible for managing a broad range of Palestinian affairs, from the judicial to the educational. Not surprisingly, the resources of the SMC and its vast patronage network became the focus of bitter rivalry, not only pitting one notable family against another, but intensifying rivalries within families as well. In his attempt to shore up his position against rivals, Hajj Amin eagerly used Islam to promote his leadership of the burgeoning Palestinian nationalist movement.

Though demonized by his Jewish and British enemies, Hajj Amin al-Husayni in fact cooperated well enough with the mandate administration. Only gradually did he use his religious authority to achieve a position of significant political influence contrary to British interests. It was a potent mix. The key event in this transformation was the so-called 'Western Wall riots' in 1929. The Western Wall was the only revealed section of what remained from the massive retaining wall built by Herod. This wall allowed Herod to enlarge the platform on which the Second Temple stood before being destroyed in AD 70. Given this association, the wall became Judaism's most important place of pilgrimage and prayer. The wall also was part of a Muslim religious trust (*waqf*): Muslim attachment to the wall and to the al-Haram al-Sharif (or 'Noble Sanctuary', as the Temple Mount is known in Arabic) is due to their association with the story of Muhammad's night journey to heaven. The wall is known to Muslims as *al-Buraq*, because Muhammad tethered his horse there, and the Dome of the Rock and the al-Aqsa mosque, built in the 7th century, are two of Islam's most revered buildings.

In 1928, attempts by some Jews to extend their access to the wall by bringing screens and benches were fiercely challenged by Hajj Amin, no doubt as part of a larger political campaign to enhance his national status. Claims and counterclaims became increasingly heated over the following year and, when a Revisionist Party youth movement organized a demonstration demanding Jewish control over the whole complex, tensions spiralled out of control. Rioting broke out in Jerusalem in August 1929, the British struggled to restore order, and the violence spread to Hebron, Jaffa, and Safad, cities with significant Jewish populations. The massacre of Jews in Hebron was especially horrifying, and those who survived fled Hebron in the wake of the riots. Overall, 133 Jews and 116 Arabs lost their lives. Palestinians worried that the Jews were violating the sanctity of Islam and dispossessing them of their patrimony. Jews compared Hebron to the pogroms of Eastern Europe.

Prelude to revolt

The tensions over access to the Western Wall galvanized the communal hostilities generated during the first decade of the mandate. In effect, they ended any real chance of Arab–Jewish peace in Palestine. Britain struggled to deal with the fallout The Shaw commission, sent out to report on the 1929 disturbances, criticized Hajj Amin al-Husayni's lack of restraint but acquitted him of incitement. More significantly, the commission warned against continued Jewish immigration and land purchase, arguing that the further dispossession of Arab farmers could only lead to more disturbances. In October 1930 the British issued the Passfield White Paper, stressing the need to deal more forthrightly with Arab concerns. It called for restrictions on Jewish immigration and land purchase and drew attention to the conspicuous absence of a representative legislative council. Zionist leaders were furious. In London, they voiced strong criticism of the White Paper and succeeded the following year in persuading the prime minister, Ramsay MacDonald, to write a personal letter to Weizmann in which key elements of the 1930 White Paper were revoked.

Palestinian Arabs, in turn, were outraged by such external lobbying, in which political factors in London seemed paramount. The 1930s would be a period when Palestine's Arab neighbours—first Iraq, then Egypt and Syria—negotiated various forms of self-government and formal independence, just as was called for by the mandate system. The Palestinians, by contrast, were no closer to self-rule. As the possibilities of constitutional change grew dimmer, the Arab notables, some of whom had a stake in continued British patronage, began to lose the confidence of their own constituencies. Increasingly Palestinian Arabs began to assert themselves as a national community. As resentment of the mandate rose, nationalist sentiment became more radicalized and more interlaced with religion. One prominent example of the sort of clandestine violence that emerged in this period is the secret armed band that formed under the leadership of a Syrian immigrant religious preacher named Shaykh 'Izz al-Din al-Qassam. Though his movement was short-lived, his attacks on Jewish settlements in the northern valleys attracted support among both the poor rural population and the marginalized urban inhabitants living in the shanty towns of Haifa, where al-Qassam was based.

In the spring and summer of 1936, after almost twenty years of British dominance, Palestine spontaneously erupted into mass demonstrations. The notables were caught off guard. They desperately tried to take the reins of popular reactions that risked spiralling out of their control. Leaders of rival factions belatedly came together in April to form a coalition, known as the Arab Higher Committee (AHC), and tried to coordinate a national strike. Unprecedented as a national effort, the strike forced both the *Yishuv* and the British to respond in significant ways. While the strike aimed to harm the *Yishuv*, it was the Arab economy that suffered worse by, in effect, accelerating the process of segregation. The *Yishuv* took advantage of the unstable situation by becoming more self-reliant and, for example, building a new port for Tel Aviv, the new Jewish city bordering Jaffa. Britain responded to the Arab demonstrations with carrot and stick, first sending 20,000 new troops to put down the rebellion and then pledging to establish (yet again) an official commission of enquiry, this one chaired by Lord Peel.

The general strike, which lasted six months, was called off by the AHC in October, ostensibly due to the mediation of neighbouring Arab states and their call for the Palestinians to trust in the commission (though it also allowed the large landowning elite to export their citrus harvest). As a precursor to future dynamics, some Arab leaders, such as the kings of Saudi Arabia and Iraq, sought to bolster their own legitimacy by involving themselves in the affairs of 'our sons the Arabs of Palestine'. Others, though, such as Abdullah of Transjordan, had ambitions of their own in Palestine itself. Palestine was opening something of a new chapter with the intervention of Arab neighbours. An even greater watershed in the unfolding of the Palestinian–Israeli conflict would come with the publication in 1937 of the Peel Commission's report. Calling for Palestine to be partitioned into separate Arab and Jewish states, the report gave rise to greater and more sustained violence.

Conclusion

In taking on the dual obligation of the mandate, Britain assumed the problematic balancing act was one it could uphold. This gross misjudgement would come back to haunt the British government. As the British imperial historian Elizabeth Monroe concluded, 'Measured by British interests alone, it is one of the greatest mistakes of our imperial history.' That the vague terms of the Balfour Declaration would, in the end, prove problematic had been foreseen by Lord Curzon back in 1917 when outlining his opposition to the whole idea: 'we ought at least to consider,' he had stressed, 'whether we are encouraging a practicable idea, or preparing the way for disappointment and failure'.

If British attempts to settle a European population among indigenous inhabitants with whom there could be no accommodation constituted one of the most problematic challenges for the Empire, the alliance born of the Balfour Declaration also proved fraught for Zionism. Zionism's close relationship with the European power ruling Palestine could not but, in the minds of the Palestinian Arabs, indelibly frame it as a settler colonial movement. For some Jewish leaders, who saw their own national liberation movement as a return to the land of their ancestors (or at least to the nearest plains and valleys), this was obviously contrary to the identity they might otherwise have wished to create in Palestine. For other leaders, however, the alliance with the British Empire was in fact key to their portrayal of the Zionist project as part of a European civilizing mission. Weizmann, for example, preferred that Jews not be referred to as a 'native population'; Herzl described the Jewish homeland as a European rampart against barbarism; Zionists commonly referred to their settlements as colonies. It is true that Colonial Secretary Winston Churchill declared in 1922 that the Jews were in Palestine as of right and not on sufferance, but Palestinian Arabs did not see the promise of a national home as Britain's to make.

Chapter 3
Palestine partitioned 1937–47

Despite the essential support offered by the British administration, when the *Yishuv* proclaimed statehood in 1948, Britain was widely portrayed as the enemy from whom independence was wrested in a war of liberation. To properly understand the radical transformations that would ultimately occur in Palestine, one needs to focus particularly close attention on the ten-year period following the 1937 Peel partition plan and the outbreak of a peasant-led Arab rebellion that would be brutally repressed by British force. If it was the First World War that broke the Ottoman Empire, the Second World War hastened the demise of the British Empire that had taken its place. The Second World War produced a 'perfect storm' of regional and international pressures whose mutually reinforcing effects served to accelerate the end of colonial rule in Palestine (thus helping to explain why this is the one chapter to treat a span of only ten rather than twenty years).

Between 1937 and 1947, Britain effectively lost control of an increasingly chaotic situation in Palestine. The Arab revolt was put down in 1939, but at great cost. British suppression inflicted tremendous damage on Palestinian political and social structures, and forced Britain to back away from the 1937 Peel partition scheme. The stick was accompanied by some carrot. With the revolt defeated, Britain attempted to conciliate Arab opposition, going so far as to reverse the commitment made to the Jews in the

Balfour Declaration. In 1939 Britain issued a new White Paper calling for an independent Palestinian state under majority Arab rule. But the war against Nazi Germany, during which Palestine became an important military base, forced Britain again to change its policies. In the wake of the Second World War, and faced with tremendous international (especially US) pressure to allow Jewish survivors of the Holocaust to enter Palestine forthwith, Britain stepped back from the 1939 White Paper's plan for an independent Palestine. In 1947 discussion returned to the question of partition, this time under the rubric of the United Nations (UN). Less than ten years earlier, Britain had agonized over the prospect of partitioning Palestine and concluded that it was the last thing they would do. And so it was.

1937 Peel Commission Report and the 1939 White Paper

As was discussed in the last chapter, conflicts over a legislative assembly, immigration, and land purchase all contributed to the growth of Arab resistance to Zionism during the interwar period. In 1936, after twenty years of colonial dominance, an Arab general strike was organized to oppose British policies. These protests were accompanied in the countryside by sporadic attacks on Jewish and British positions. Sometimes referred to as the first phase of the Arab revolt, the six-month strike was brought to an end in October 1936 when the Palestinian leadership, made up of members of notable families who had finally come together as a national body known as the Arab Higher Committee (AHC), accepted Britain's plan to appoint a new commission. Chaired by Lord William Robert Peel, former Secretary of State for India, this commission joined the ever-growing list of official investigations into causes of unrest in Palestine. Its report published in the following year would make it the most famous.

Officially entitled the Palestine Royal Commission, the Peel Commission was dispatched to determine whether 'either the

Arabs or the Jews have any legitimate grievances' and, if so, 'to make recommendations for their removal and for the prevention of their recurrence'. Though tasked with finding a way to fit two national movements into a single territory, the commission instead concluded that they were irreconcilable, a Gordian knot that could only be cut by the sword.

THE PALESTINE ROYAL (PEEL) COMMISSION REPORT, July 1937

[T]he Mandate cannot be fully and honourably implemented unless by some means or other the national antagonism between Arab and Jew can be composed. But it is the Mandate that created that antagonism and keeps it alive; and, as long as the Mandate exists, we cannot honestly hold out the expectation that either Arabs or Jews will be able to set aside their national hopes or fears and sink their differences in the common service of Palestine. That being so, real 'self-governing institutions' cannot be developed, nor can the Mandate ever terminate, without violating its obligations, general or specific. For at any given time there must be either an Arab or a Jewish majority in Palestine, and the government of an independent Palestine, freed from the Mandate, would have to be either an Arab or a Jewish government. In the latter event—assuming, we repeat, that the miracle of reconciliation has not happened and that politics are still conducted on lines of race—the general obligation implicit in all Mandates that the people entrusted to Mandatory administration are to be enabled in course of time to 'stand by themselves' would not have been fulfilled. In the other event, the obligation in Article 2 'for placing the country under such political, administrative and economic conditions as will secure the establishment of the Jewish National Home' would not have been discharged.

. . .

> Manifestly the problem cannot be solved by giving either the Arabs or the Jews all they want. The answer to the question 'Which of them in the end will govern Palestine?' must surely be 'Neither'. We do not think that any fair-minded statesman would suppose, now that the hope of harmony between the races has proved untenable, that Britain ought either to hand over to Arab rule 400,000 Jews, whose entry into Palestine has been for the most part facilitated by the British Government and approved by the League of Nations; or that, if the Jews should become a majority, a million or so of Arabs should be handed over to their rule. But, while neither race can justly rule all Palestine, we see no reason why, if it were practicable, each race should not rule part of it.

The commission's report was published in July 1937, accompanied by a map proposing new boundaries for a reconstructed Palestine (see Illustration 6). In its view, partition was best brought about by the emergence of a Jewish state in the agriculturally rich coastal plain in the west and the hills in the north. Peel's partition map was thus influenced by modern Zionist settlement patterns, not ancient Biblical identifications. It is also important to note that the proposed Jewish state would be home to a very large Arab minority, almost half the proposed state's population (by contrast, in the area allotted to the Arab state there were only some 1,200 Jews). The Peel Commission believed that for the partition to be 'clean and final', the question of the large Arab minority must be 'boldly faced and firmly dealt with'. So, as a necessary corollary to partition, Peel called for an 'exchange of population': that is, the transfer of over 200,000 Arabs in order to make room for a Jewish state. Some areas (including Jerusalem, Bethlehem, and a corridor to the Mediterranean) would remain under British control. As for the remaining area of Palestine, about 80 per cent, the Peel plan recommended that it be united with the neighbouring Emirate of Transjordan. Its Hashemite ruler, Abdullah, welcomed the idea.

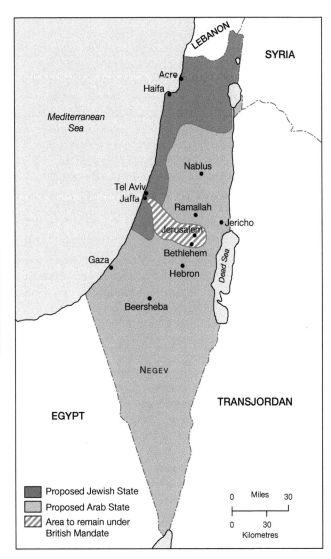

6. The 1937 Peel Commission partition plan

The Zionist response to the Peel recommendations was somewhat equivocal. At the twentieth Zionist Congress, held at Zurich in August 1937, Chaim Weizmann and David Ben Gurion together promoted partition against those who refused to give up the Zionist claim to more territory (including, in the case of the Revisionists, Transjordan). By accepting Peel's idea of partition, the pragmatic Zionist leadership was not necessarily registering its agreement to Peel's detailed allotment of territory. When questioned about the wisdom of dividing the south from the proposed state, Weizmann responded: 'It will not run away.' In the end, the delegates sought endorsement for the principle of a Jewish state, voting strategically in favour of partition but rejecting the plan.

While some British officials came around to seeing Peel's partition plan as the most hopeful solution to an intractable problem, others were wary of imposing such hardship on the indigenous Arab population. It was widely understood that the idea of transferring thousands of Arab families from the lands of their ancestors, as recommended by Peel, could only happen through the use of force. The British government decided to appoint a 'technical' commission to sort out the logistics of implementing the partition plan, and it ended up repudiating the proposal. Forced transfer of the Arab population was considered a non-starter. Yet without such recourse the prospect of a Jewish state including such a large Arab minority presented a future source of insoluble problems. Thus, insuperable as the difficulties of continuing the mandate seemed to the Peel Commission, the British government, upon further examination and reflection, deemed partition even less workable.

As for the Arab response to the Peel partition proposals, it was marked by the eruption of one of the most significant anti-colonial revolts ever confronted by the British Empire.

Although the goals of the 1937–9 revolt remained the same as in 1936, the nature of Arab protest changed. Britain declared the AHC illegal in October 1937 and issued warrants for the arrest and deportation of leading notables. Lacking a central system of command, the revolt was fought by thousands of peasants, mostly in the hill areas of Palestine's central and northern regions. Operations were frequently undertaken at night, while farming continued, as best it could, during the day. By the summer of 1938, rebel attacks on British positions (such as police stations and railways) had completely disrupted the government's capacity to provide services. Increasingly the peasants' anger was also directed towards their own notable class. Where possible, rebel leaders demanded financial 'donations' from the wealthy landowners and cancelled the payment of rents and debts. It was during this period that the *keffiyeh*—the popular head cloth, tied with a black headband, worn by peasants—became the patriotic symbol of Palestinian identity. Though in a state of near civil war, Palestinian national identity had never before been so forcefully expressed.

Rebels also targeted Jewish property. The besieged *Yishuv* responded by strengthening both its determination and its capacity to become independent. For example, 'Special Night Squads' were created in 1938 under the guidance of Orde Wingate, a British soldier who within weeks of his arrival in Palestine zealously embraced Zionism. Wingate commanded small-scale operations to retaliate fiercely against Arab guerrilla attacks as well as to defend the Iraq oil pipeline that ended in Haifa. Meanwhile Jewish militias such as the Irgun grew and gained strength.

By 1939, the revolt was cruelly crushed by British imperial authorities. Deploying over 20,000 soldiers, the British pursued a brutal policy of destruction and collective punishment. The consequences in Palestine were profound: 10 per cent of the Palestinian male population were reported to have been killed, wounded, imprisoned, or exiled; thousands of houses were destroyed; social structures were fractured and the economy reduced to chaos. At the political level, colonial political and administrative structures dissolved under the strain. Notables who were represented on the AHC were either deported or fled into exile.

At the diplomatic level, the high toll of suppressing the revolt brought about a dramatic change in British plans for governing Palestine. Britain accepted the need to review the mandate and reconsider its support for building a Jewish national home in Palestine against the will of the Arab majority. Reinterpretations of the ambiguous Balfour Declaration lay at the centre of official debates at this time. Some officials stressed the provision for the protection of Arab interests; some argued that the obligations to build 'a national home' for the Jewish people had in fact now been redeemed; and some had become thoroughly disillusioned or worn down by the widespread accusations of betrayal coming from all sides. A particularly important consideration at this time was the prospect of war with Germany and the need to secure Britain's communications and supply routes.

Abandoning the idea of partition, London issued in 1939 a new White Paper that dealt individually with the three major issues of contention: immigration, land, and a constitution. Laying down limits on Jewish immigration, the White Paper announced that Jewish immigration would be restricted to 75,000 persons over a five-year period and then end (or, technically, be subject to the acquiescence of the Arab majority). Furthermore, the White Paper restricted the continued purchase of land by Zionists to specific geographical zones. Most importantly, the White Paper called for the establishment of a unitary Palestinian state in which Arabs and Jews would jointly exercise authority. It contemplated needing ten years to bring about an independent Palestinian state. But it was in this coming decade that Britain rapidly lost control of the situation in Palestine.

The Second World War and the Holocaust

The Second World War had an enormous impact on Palestine. The political landscape was completely transformed. Not only was Britain thoroughly distracted during the course of the war from implementing the constitutional recommendations of the White Paper, but by the end of the conflict it was also so weakened that it simply lacked the will and capacity to determine for itself Palestine's future. The Palestinians too were depleted and exhausted. Still reeling from the brutal suppression of the Arab revolt, and further compromised by Hajj Amin al-Husayni's attempt to seek assistance from Nazi Germany, the Palestinians lacked strong leadership. From exile, the largely discredited Mufti had failed to rally fellow Palestinian Arabs to support the Nazis, though his stubborn rejection of the 1939 White Paper, aimed above all at securing his own leadership, succeeded in intimidating anyone else from effectively negotiating with the British.

The two main factors that gravely undermined Britain's post-war position in Palestine were the power of the *Yishuv* and the influence of the United States. The *Yishuv* had deeply resented the 1939 White Paper and its plan to curtail immigration to Palestine just when European Jewry was most in need of sanctuary. But the Zionists still needed British patronage, and the subsequent outbreak of war made it imperative for Zionist leaders to support the British war against Germany. The Zionist response is best captured in David Ben Gurion's famous call: 'We will fight the war as if there was no White Paper and fight the White Paper as if there was no war.' In the end, Zionist cooperation with the Allied war effort provided the *Yishuv* with an opportunity to both strengthen its military capabilities and build up, if secretly, its store of armaments. As the horrors of the Holocaust, in which six million European Jews would perish, gradually became known, Zionist resolve to create an independent state hardened. In May 1942 a conference was held at the Biltmore Hotel in New York

City, the location itself representing the growing influence of the United States. The programme called for a Jewish state over the whole of Palestine, replacing the idea of a 'home' in part of it, and this remained official policy until 1947. Meanwhile, on the ground, British authorities were up against the by now unstoppable Jewish push, including brutal attacks by extremist factions calling for an independent state. Revisionist organizations such as the Irgun and the Stern Gang directed their attacks on British personnel, most famously assassinating Lord Moyne, the British minister of state resident in the Middle East, in November 1944 and in July 1946 demolishing a wing of Jerusalem's King David Hotel where British administrative headquarters were based. Britain responded to these increasing hostilities by deploying 80,000 troops and 20,000 policemen, all to deal with a population in the *Yishuv* of approximately 600,000.

Following the Second World War, many countries, especially in the West, declared their full support for an independent Jewish state as a home for Jewish refugees who had survived the Holocaust. Most acutely, Britain faced a growing rift with the US President, Harry Truman, and his constant demand—driven in part by overwhelming sympathy for the plight of Jewish refugees and in part by domestic electoral politics—for the relaxation of the 1939 White Paper and the immediate entry into Palestine of 100,000 Jewish immigrants. It was a critical moment. Given the war weariness and financial destitution felt at home, Britain urgently needed US support and financial aid in order to retain any hope of maintaining its status as a great power.

British withdrawal and the 1947 UN partition plan

Historians agree that all of these issues led Britain in February 1947 to turn for help to the UN, the successor to the League of Nations and its flawed mandate system. But the exact nature of that decision is the source of some debate. Some view this turn to the UN as less an act of desperation than part of a longer-term strategy to secure British interests in Palestine while smoothing relations with the United States. According to this interpretation, Britain essentially challenged the body of world opinion either to come up with a responsible plan (and supply the forces necessary to bring it about) or to come around to supporting Britain's actions (and leave it alone). Other historians, however, find no reason to view Britain's decision as anything other than an attempt to wash its hands of an impossible and demoralizing problem. Having had enough of bearing the spiralling cost all by itself, Britain was now looking for someone else to take responsibility.

Either way, handing over the problem of Palestine to the UN effectively introduced a new factor into the equation. The situation changed markedly once the UN set up a special committee on Palestine, known as UNSCOP (United Nations Special Committee on Palestine). UNSCOP's wide terms of reference, which called for the future of Palestine to be determined in connection with the problem of Europe's displaced Jews, angered the Palestinian Arab leadership. They argued that it was unfair to view Palestine as part of the solution for a European problem. When UNSCOP visited Palestine in June and July of 1947, Arab delegates refused officially to meet it, and their uncompromising leadership was again portrayed as constituting their own worst enemy. It was also evident, however, that Arab leaders were hamstrung by the unique absence in Palestine of a legislative assembly that would have granted Palestinian representatives, had they been serving as ministers of an elected government, much greater legitimacy in pressing their case for sovereignty.

In addition to the legacy of constitutional impasse emerging from the mandate period, the issues of Jewish immigration and land purchase also loomed large. By far the most eventful moment of UNSCOP's visit to Palestine was the arrival in Haifa of 4,500 Jewish displaced persons crammed into a boat renamed *Exodus*.

UNSCOP Report to the General Assembly, 1947

In making its proposal for a plan of partition with economic union for Palestine, the members of the Committee supporting this plan are fully aware of the many difficulties of effecting a satisfactory division of Palestine into a Jewish and an Arab State. The main problems to be faced are the following:

1. The problem of minorities

The central inland area of Palestine includes a large Arab population and, leaving Jerusalem out of account, practically no Jews. This obviously is the main starting point in demarcating a possible Arab State. Further north, particularly in Western Galilee, and separated from the central area by a narrow belt of Jewish settlements, is another concentration of Arabs and very few Jews. These two areas form the main territory of an Arab State which has only a very small minority of Jews. The Jewish State, on the other hand, has its centre and starting point in the coastal plain between Haifa and Tel Aviv and even in this area there is also a considerable number of Arabs. Extensions of this area in the most suitable directions to include a larger number of Jews as well as a larger land area, increase the proportion of Arabs to Jews in the Jewish State.

2. The problem of viability

The creation of two viable States is considered essential to a partition scheme.

3. The problem of development

A partition scheme for Palestine must take into account both the claims of the Jews to receive immigrants and the needs of the Arab population, which is increasing rapidly by natural means. Thus, as far as possible, both partitioned States must leave some room for further land settlement.

4. The problem of contiguity

It is obviously desirable to create States with continuous frontiers. Due to geographic and demographic factors, it is impossible to make a satisfactory partition without sacrificing this objective to some extent.

5. Access to the sea for the Arab State

Even within the scheme for economic union, this is considered to be important for psychological as well as material reasons.

In solving this complex of problems, a compromise is necessary and in suggesting the boundaries upon which this partition scheme rests all these matters have been given serious consideration so that the solution finally reached appears to be the least unsatisfactory from most points of view.

UNSCOP members watched as British officials, upholding the policies of the 1939 White Paper, sent the captured illegal immigrants back to Europe, the continent of their persecution. Indeed, the dark shadow cast by the Holocaust ensured that UNSCOP members framed the partitioning of Palestine and the creation of new frontiers for a Jewish state in moral terms. As Ivan Rand, the Canadian committee member who as a representative of one of Britain's 'loyal dominions' might otherwise have been expected to sympathize with British policy, told David Horowitz, a UN correspondent and ardent Zionist: 'I won't allow you to be placed in a territorial ghetto.'

Though united in calling for an end to the British mandate, UNSCOP submitted a majority and a minority report. The minority report, which called for the establishment of a single federated state, attracted little attention. The majority report, supported by eight of the eleven members, revived the idea of partitioning Palestine raised ten years earlier by the Peel Commission. It outlined the terms of partition and prepared the way for the UN General Assembly to vote in November 1947. A watershed in the history of the conflict, the UN vote was both controversial and indeterminate. To achieve the required approval of a two-thirds majority in the General Assembly, extensive lobbying was undertaken. The Zionist campaign was also helped enormously by the singular appearance of Soviet-US harmony. Soviet endorsement of partition emerged out of both a feeling of sympathy for Jewish suffering and a cold calculation of how best to undermine Britain in this strategically important region. In many official circles Palestine came to be regarded as a test case of whether the new UN was to be a more effective world organization than the League of Nations, and people desperately wanted the UN to work. On 29 November the tally in the General Assembly was thirty-three to thirteen in favour of partition, with ten abstentions (including Britain).

The 1947 UN plan was officially entitled 'Resolution 181 (II) Future Government of Palestine'. It proposed the partitioning of the unitary state of Palestine into two countries, one Jewish and one Arab, and the establishment of a special international regime over the Jerusalem area and its religious sites. UNSCOP went much further than the Peel Commission in accommodating Zionist aims. On paper, the areas proposed for the Jewish state comprised 55 per cent of Palestine's territory, including vital water supplies, most citrus plantations (both Arab and Jewish), and the largely unpopulated Negev desert, even though Jews constituted only 33 per cent of Palestine's population and owned less than 10 per cent of the total land area. This inequitable distribution was determined in large part by the anticipated need of the new Jewish state to absorb hundreds of thousands of Holocaust survivors. The population embraced by the proposed frontiers of the projected Jewish state comprised approximately 500,000 Jews and a very large minority of 400,000 Arabs. The proposed Arab state, on the other hand, was almost entirely Arab.

Partition plans are, by their very nature, offensive and destructive. In the valleys and plains of western and northern Palestine, Jewish settlements and Arab villages were thoroughly intermingled. There simply was no way of drawing straightforward boundaries that brought together the largely urban Jewish populations without including a large proportion of the Arab population. Instead of aiming for contiguity, the UN proposal, as shown in Illustration 7, envisaged each state consisting of three separate parts, creating a criss-cross arrangement with two meeting points where the Jewish and Arab territorial units would overlap. The unnatural borders separating the Arab and Jewish territories were described by George Kirk as an entwining of the two communities 'in an inimical embrace like two fighting serpents'.

Jewish land acquisition during the mandate period played the key role in determining the contours of UNSCOP's proposed Jewish state. As has been shown in previous chapters, a combination of economic, legal, and political processes had significant implications for the settlement patterns of Jewish immigrants. Jewish land purchasers gravitated towards Palestine's more agriculturally productive coastal plains and inland valleys where settlers could focus on building citrus plantations. This notable shift in the definition of the Jewish homeland had an important impact on the drawing of new political boundaries aimed at partitioning the land. UNSCOP's proposed borders for a Jewish state aimed only at consolidating the various districts in Palestine with the highest relative percentage of Jewish holdings (plus the southern Negev desert). As a result, the central mountainous areas of Biblical antiquity, known to Jews as Judea and Samaria, ended up being located in the areas designated for a Palestinian Arab state.

Although arrangements were made for a UN commission to oversee the transfer of administrative powers to two new states, the commission achieved nothing. Its failure was due in part to lack of

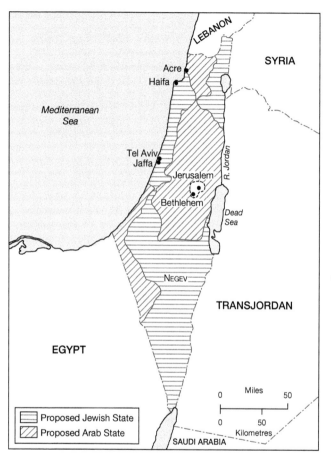

7. **The 1947 UN partition plan**

resources and in part to Britain's refusal to cooperate in any way. Britain was not prepared to implement a plan that would both damage its wider objectives in the Arab world and result in further sacrifices. It had responded to the UNSCOP report by announcing its decision to withdraw entirely by 15 May 1948, leaving the UN to figure out how to carry out its own schemes: the last British chief secretary in Palestine would leave the keys to his office under the mat. 'Experiment in anarchy' is how Richard Graves, a senior British official in Jerusalem during the troubled last months of mandatory rule, described the chaos into which Palestine had been plunged: 'the contestants who are supposed to have had their cause settled in a court of law will be left to fight it out'.

Conclusion

Following the Second World War the *Yishuv* became a state-in-the-making and Britain, with its diminishing resources vastly overstretched, could not succeed in fighting the militant Zionist campaign. The world's indignation had been aroused by British efforts to prevent Jewish survivors from entering Palestine. The tragedy of the Holocaust had become a deep source of emotive power and moral conviction, for both Zionists and non-Zionists: the world's sympathy was now with the idea of recognizing a Jewish state where the Jewish people could be safe from a repetition of the horrors of the death camps. Nor could Britain, wholly dependent on US aid as it adjusted to a new international climate, afford a confrontation with the United States and the external pressure it exerted to allow for greater immigration.

In the fighting that began on the morning after the UN vote, 'Palestine' disappeared from the map. For reasons discussed in the following chapter, the proposed Palestinian Arab state never came into being. Many observers blame the Palestinians themselves, and its leadership's history of continually rejecting proposals preferable in hindsight to the solutions that would be presented afterwards. Their counterfactual assumption is that, had Palestinians accepted the 1947 UN partition plan or the 1937 Peel Commission, the territory on which Palestinians would gain independence would have been much larger.

In this vein, it has also been argued that Palestinian rejection of the 1923 legislative assembly (see Chapter 2) was the largest of the missed opportunities: had the proposed constitutional machinery been accepted, Palestine, and Palestinians, would have been represented by a semblance of legislative government that would have made the post-Second World War task of partition vastly more difficult. Indeed, Palestine, the only Middle Eastern state not to have a legislative assembly during the interwar period, remains the only one to have been partitioned. However mistaken Palestinian rejectionism can be seen to have been in hindsight, one must nonetheless try to understand the factors that contributed to it. One was the evident unfairness of the political offers and the widely held feeling that better ones had to be achieved. Second was the apparent failure of the leadership of the notables: fierce rivalries between, and among, competing family members undermined the attempts by individual Palestinian leaders who saw the need to negotiate, but feared the opportunity it presented to their opponents to vilify them for compromising.

When the fighting ended in 1949, the armistice lines carved out for the new state of Israel added much more territory than had been envisaged by the UN plan. The new state now comprised 78 per cent of the land of mandate Palestine. It was not until the 1987 *intifada* that the Palestinian leadership officially embraced Palestinian statehood as conceived by the partition solution—that is, ceding to Israel the 78 per cent of Palestine on which it was created. By the terms of that compromise, Palestinians accepted what remained of the UN plan to partition Palestine, but they would insist on 100 per cent of that 22 per cent.

Chapter 4
Atzmaut and *Nakba* 1947–67

In 1947 the United Nations (UN) mapped out new boundaries for the mandate territory. Its plan awarded over half of the land, including the fertile plains and valleys, to the *Yishuv* who at the time made up one-third of the population. In Palestine, the day following the vote was marked, understandably enough, by Jews rejoicing and Arabs bitterly protesting. When the situation deteriorated into a civil war, international observers began to worry about what would come next. Diplomatic efforts at the UN to secure the implementation of the plan were futile. Many delegates were distressed by Britain's refusal to help impose the partition plan, but Britain officially held that those who had voted for it ought to step up and face the consequences. Secretly, British officials tended to favour the absorption by Transjordan of the mountainous parts of the UN's proposed Palestinian Arab state. With events spinning out of control on Britain's watch, the United States became increasingly worried about the violence and instability; in March 1948 the Truman administration shifted away from partition, advocating instead for a temporary international trusteeship. But the unravelling had already gone too far.

Fighting on the ground broke out on two fronts. First, from November 1947 to May 1948, there was a civil war within Palestine between the *Yishuv* and Palestinian Arab society.

Secondly, following the final withdrawal of British forces on 15 May 1948, a regional war broke out between the new state of Israel and its Arab neighbours. Egypt, Transjordan, Syria, Lebanon, and Iraq sent expeditionary forces, while token contingents were also dispatched from Saudi Arabia and Yemen. By the time armistice agreements were signed in early to mid 1949, the independent state of Israel was established within expanded boundaries that comprised 78 per cent of mandate Palestine, including the western part of Jerusalem (see Illustration 8). Israel's victory was hailed by the Jews as the War of Independence (in Hebrew, *milhemet ha'atzmaut*), a revolutionary overthrow of the British imperial yoke and a hard-fought victory over the new state's Arab enemies. The 6,000 deaths suffered by the *Yishuv* constituted 1 per cent of its population. Convinced by the justice of Zionism, and proud of their resounding victory, Israelis celebrated a heroic end to centuries of suffering and powerlessness in the diaspora. For the next two decades, the state of Israel focused its attention on economic consolidation, the absorption of another wave of immigrants (which doubled its Jewish population within three years), and maintaining its defences against belligerent Arab neighbours.

In contrast, Palestinian Arab society was largely destroyed, its population dispersed throughout the region. During the course of the fighting, approximately 750,000 Palestinians fled or were expelled from their homes. It was an unimaginable catastrophe (in Arabic, *al-nakba*) that became synonymous with their dispossession and expulsion from the land of their ancestors. Their suffering as refugees set the primary context for the evolution of Palestinian national identity. Denied the right to return to their homes, Palestinian refugees deeply resented Israel's hurried efforts to develop and settle their former lands, and some fought to obstruct it. But, until the 1967 war, the international community viewed Palestinians more as a humanitarian problem than as autonomous political actors.

Area assigned to a Jewish state in the plan

Area assigned to an Arab state in the plan

Area assigned to a 'corpus separatum' (neither Jewish nor Arab) in plan

Israel in the 1949 armistice lines

Controlled by Egypt and Jordan from 1949 to 1967

Comparison of the United Nations General Assembly partition plan of 29 November 1947 (Resolution 181) and the armistice lines of 1949

Miles
0   50

0   50
Kilometres

8. **The 1949 UN armistice lines**

The Palestinian defeat in the 1947–9 fighting transformed the conflict from a struggle between the Arab and Jewish inhabitants of Palestine into also an interstate rivalry widely referred to as the Arab–Israeli conflict. In the most populous Arab states, this period was a time of great domestic instability. Arab regimes would be so discredited by the losses inflicted on their armies that ruling elites were swept aside in rapid succession. In addition to bitter self-criticism, the defeat also intensified Arab anger against the Western powers that had fragmented the Arab world after the First World War and then supported Zionism. As was happening around the world, the process of European decolonization offered opportunities to the two new superpowers, the United States and the Soviet Union, to expand their influence during the 1950s and 1960s. The tension-ridden armistices of 1949 led to renewed rounds of fighting which played a decisive role in embroiling the Middle East in the Cold War competition for global supremacy.

Nakba: Palestinian catastrophe

Reeling from the losses suffered during the 1937–9 revolt, and still paralysed by political factionalism, Palestinian Arabs lacked the necessary political and military structures with which to confront the well coordinated forces of the *Yishuv*. When intercommunal clashes broke out in the winter of 1947–8, many Arabs, especially the wealthy and middle-class families, fled the fighting, with plans to return once the situation was safe again. Then, in April 1948, *Haganah* authorized a campaign known as Plan D, which gave *Haganah* officers authority to undertake the 'destruction and expulsion or occupation' of Arab villages, as deemed necessary to secure the interior of the emergent Jewish state. In effect, the atrocities that occurred during the implementation of Plan D intensified the fears of the Arab population and led to the irreversible momentum of panicked flight from successive villages and towns. Among the most notorious attacks was the killing in April 1948 of over a hundred Palestinian residents in the village of Deir Yassin by Irgun and Stern Gang extremists. Within days,

Arab fighters retaliated by killing almost eighty members of a Jewish armed medical convoy on its way to Mount Scopus, on the edge of Jerusalem. As news of such massacres was widely broadcast, fears of further retribution and atrocities forced more Arabs to flee their homes in territories under Jewish control.

Of the 750,000 refugees, approximately 400,000 fled to Jordan and 150,000 crossed the borders to Lebanon and Syria (see Illustration 9). Meanwhile, 200,000 refugees found themselves enclosed in a small strip of land—approximately 50 kms in length and 6-12 kms in width (360 km^2)—around Gaza, which was already home to 80,000 residents. In December 1948, the UN General Assembly passed Resolution 194 recognizing the refugees' right to return to their homes. In December 1949, the United Nations Relief and Works Agency (UNRWA) was established to provide temporary assistance in the refugee camps. The Palestinians who had fled the fighting expected to return home once it had ended. But Israel refused to let them do so, arguing that the Arab states had been responsible for creating the problem by initiating hostilities. In the absence of a political resolution, their numbers kept growing. Today the number of registered UNRWA refugees is over four million. UNRWA, for its part, continues to provide assistance for housing, health care, and education in the camps, which over time began to resemble permanent townships and shanty towns.

For both political and economic reasons, Arab host states have failed to integrate the Palestinian refugees in any meaningful way. Lebanon, whose government was highly apprehensive about fundamentally altering the country's complex sectarian balance, placed the strictest regulations with regard to residence, travel, and employment. The Egyptian army effectively imposed emergency law in Gaza, though Syria was more relaxed in its approach to the refugees and provided for some support and integration. The only country to grant citizenship was Jordan (Transjordan became Jordan in March 1948), which did so as part

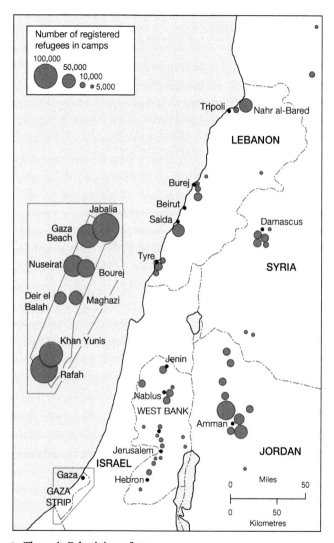

Number of registered refugees in camps

100,000 50,000 10,000 5,000

Tripoli · Nahr al-Bared

LEBANON

Burej
Beirut
Saida

Tyre

Damascus

SYRIA

Jabalia
Gaza Beach
Nuseirat
Bourej
Deir el Balah
Maghazi
Khan Yunis
Rafah

Jenin

Nablus
WEST BANK

Amman

Jerusalem

ISRAEL

Hebron

JORDAN

Gaza

GAZA STRIP

Miles
0   50

0   50
Kilometres

Atzmaut and Nakba 1947–67

9. The main Palestinian refugee camps

59

of its absorption of Palestinian territory. Although Jordanian nationality was granted to all of its Palestinian inhabitants, in exchange Palestinians were prohibited from using the term Palestine. Officially, Jordan now had two provinces: one on the 'west bank' of the Jordan River and the other on its 'east bank'. By thus annexing Palestinian territory into his kingdom, King Abdullah was following up on the First World War ambitions of his father to establish Hashemite rule over the whole Arab east (ideas that had been further elaborated upon by the Peel Commission plan of 1937).

The main victors in the war for Palestine were Israel and Jordan. Facilitated by prior negotiations that had secretly taken place between the two sides, Israel and Jordan agreed in 1949 to armistice lines that drastically modified the 1947 UN partition plan. The mountainous area on the west bank of the Jordan River (which comprised the ancient Biblical regions of Judea and Samaria) was annexed by Jordan (and renamed as the 'West Bank'). However, neither Israel nor Jordan had wanted the UN's plan for the internationalization of Jerusalem, and the fight to control the city was fierce. By early 1949, a line of barbed wire, concrete walls, and fortified posts divided the holy city. Jordan had secured control over the old city (including the Temple Mount/al-Haram al-Sharif) while Israel held the newer parts in the western sector, with only a single road linking it to the new state of Israel. Although the UN failed miserably in its attempts to implement a *corpus separatum* for Jerusalem, as called for in the 1947 plan, the international community never recognized the de facto division of the city into western and eastern sectors.

Abdullah's success in achieving significant territorial gains speaks to the conflicting and self-serving agendas that throughout the fighting undermined pan-Arab support for Palestinians. Although all neighbouring Arab states agreed to send troops into Palestine once Britain had withdrawn, their armies were small, ill-trained and ill-equipped, and unable to coordinate military strategies.

The total number of Arab troops committed to the war was approximately 25,000, whereas the Israeli Defence Forces (official successor to *Haganah*) raised 35,000 troops. So disorganized were Arab forces that each country's army fought separately, thus allowing Israel to concentrate its forces where they were most effective. As historian Avi Shlaim concludes:

> the picture that emerges is not the familiar one of Israel standing alone against the combined might of the entire Arab world but rather one of a remarkable convergence between the interests of Israel and those of Transjordan against the other members of the Arab coalition, and especially against the Palestinians.

Abdullah was assassinated in East Jerusalem in July 1951. Indeed, the leaders of Egypt, Syria, and Iraq were all swept away in the decade that followed the war for Palestine. Removing the corrupt and self-serving elites so closely tied to the colonial era and its social and political inequities was seen as a step in avenging the 'catastrophe' of 1948. The most far-reaching of these regime changes was the military coup that in 1952 overthrew the Egyptian monarchy and brought to power Colonel Gamal Abd al-Nasser, a soldier who had personally suffered the humiliation of defeat in the Palestine war.

Atzmaut: Israeli independence

On 14 May 1948, David Ben Gurion declared Israel's independence as a 'Jewish state established by and for the Jewish people'. With both the Soviet Union and the United States quickly recognizing Israel, the new state nonetheless had to fight hard for its survival against the Arab forces which immediately attacked it. Born in a hostile regional situation, the Israeli state confronted daunting challenges, especially with regard to demography and security.

When the regional war came to an end in mid 1949, the state of Israel had a population of 800,000, of whom 160,000 (or about

20 per cent) were Palestinian Arabs who remained in, or close to, their homes. Although they were given Israeli citizenship, they were also regarded as a fifth column and placed under military government that dated back to Britain's harsh mandatory emergency regulations. Even after the military administration came to an end in 1966, certain exclusionary practices towards the Arab population continued, prominent among them budgetary inequality and the discrimination involved in being prohibited from buying or leasing land.

By the terms of the 1950 Law of Return, Israeli citizenship was guaranteed to Jews from around the world. By 1951, the population of Israel had almost doubled, to over 1.3 million. Approximately half of these new immigrants were European (Ashkenazi) Jews, and the other half Mizrahi (also known as Sephardic, or Oriental, Jews) arrived from Arab countries. The reasons behind the exodus of Jews from the Arab world were varied—some were attracted by Zionist ideals or encouraged by Israel to emigrate; others (particularly in Iraq) fled anti-Semitism and systematic persecution—but the result was the same: ancient Jewish communities in cities such as Baghdad all but disappeared. Although attempts have been made to link, as part of an overall 'population exchange', the property claims of the Mizrahi immigrants to those of the Palestinian refugees, some observers have questioned the fairness of politicizing the issue in this way. While Palestinian claims for compensation are against Israel, Jewish claims are not against Palestinians, but rather against other Arab countries, which were either not involved in the war for Palestine (Morocco, Tunisia, and Libya, for example) or were caught up in their own complex process of decolonization (for example, Algeria).

The challenge of absorbing the surge of immigrants into the new state of Israel was twofold: on the one hand, the government needed to find them housing and jobs; on the other, it sought to imbue a common sense of citizenship. Certainly, Israel's remarkable economic growth during the first decade or so smoothed the task of settling the new immigrants. The government was able to pursue highly ambitious and interventionist spending programmes thanks to the massive amount of money transferred to it in the form of donations from world Jewry, reparations for the Holocaust from the West German government, and some defence aid from countries such as France and the United States. The government's control over the urban and agricultural property that had belonged to Palestinian Arab refugees also helped a great deal, as new Jewish immigrants, for example, moved into abandoned Arab homes.

For a number of reasons, Mizrahi immigrants entered Israeli society as an underclass, alienated from the Ashkenazi elite who were overwhelmingly made up of the descendants of the second and third *aliyot* from Europe. Mizrahi Jews arrived with fewer resources, and large numbers of them were housed in the poorer urban quarters or sent to settle the new development towns along the borders. The striking gaps between Ashkenazi and Mizrahi Jews, in such areas as government representation and average per capita income, persisted until the 1970s, when the political influence exercised by the Mizrahi community eventually brought about a dramatic upheaval in Israeli politics (as witnessed in the 1977 elections).

Upon independence, the new state was determined to establish a democratic government (at least for Jews). Power was vested in the 120-seat parliament known as the Knesset. As elsewhere, the parliamentary system provided for strong party control over its members. Seats were distributed to any party that received 1 per cent (in 1992 raised to 1.5 per cent) of the votes. Given this electoral system, the parties that won the most seats typically failed to secure an absolute majority and were thus forced to build coalition governments, a process of negotiation and compromise that often disproportionately empowered smaller parties. In the first decades, David Ben Gurion's Mapai party took advantage of its strategic place near the centre of the political spectrum to form stable coalition governments with a combination of religious and leftist parties. As a result, Ben Gurion played an especially influential role in the early state-building process. For example, as a new Israeli Defence Force (IDF) was being moulded from the diversity of pre-state militias, the revisionist organization led by Menachem Begin, Irgun, continued to act independently of the new government. Determined to bring the organization to heel, Ben Gurion (who held the post of defence minister as well as prime minister) ordered the IDF to take action. In June 1948 it fired upon and sank a ship, the *Altalena*, carrying arms for the Irgun, several members of which were killed in the fighting.

The hostile atmosphere in which it was born meant that the IDF absorbed a large proportion of the nation's resources. Moreover, Israel's reserve army was based on two years of military conscription for men and one for women (raised in 1975 to three and two years respectively). In his attitude towards the Arab world, Ben Gurion adopted a highly activist approach, sometimes called 'Ben Gurionism'. Based on the belief that a constant show of Israel's military superiority would eventually force the Arab world to accept Israel's presence, this attitude ensured that no attack on Israel would go unpunished. Indeed, it was made clear that Israel would retaliate with disproportionate force. While the policy of severe retaliation may have served at some level as a deterrent, the policy also contributed to heightened enmity and a repeating cycle of violence in which both Arabs and Jews saw themselves as innocent victims acting against injustice.

'The Arab–Israeli conflict'

The two decades following the 1947–9 fighting were dominated by the interstate conflict between Israel and her Arab neighbours. The tense situation was further complicated by bitter inter-Arab rivalries centred on the assertive role played by Gamal Abd al-Nasser. During this time, Nasser came to represent throughout the Arab world a dynamic route towards a more promising regional order shorn of imperial ties. Palestinians especially looked to him as the leader to unite the Arab world against Israel.

The 1949 armistice agreements left unresolved two major sources of friction. One was the question of demarcating Israel's borders: the ceasefire lines (also known as the Green Line), which had so greatly modified the 1947 UN partition plan, were fragile and contested: some villages were cut in half; others were separated from their agricultural lands. The second question was the future of Palestinian refugees, languishing in temporary camps: many attempted to make their way through the permeable ceasefire lines either to rejoin families, harvest crops, and reclaim property, or to sabotage attempts by new Israeli immigrants to develop the land for themselves. In the face of growing violence, Israel's strategy of disproportionate retaliation targeted both the returning Palestinian refugees and the states from which they entered Israel. The mutual sense of insecurity that emerged from this unstable border situation led all sides to expect another round of fighting. And, indeed, Israeli cross-border retaliatory raids in 1953, killing sixty-nine villagers of the West Bank town of Qibya, and in 1955, killing thirty-eight Egyptian soldiers in Gaza, were followed in quick order by a series of sharp steps that would culminate in 1956 in another war.

The Gaza raid in particular so exposed Egypt's weakness that Nasser hurried to redress the evident military imbalance. Until then, the United States had been providing substantial economic aid to Egypt as part of its Cold War search for allies. The Americans hoped that Nasser would formally align with the West and join the regional anti-communist defence scheme known as the Baghdad Pact, which had been formed in 1955. Instead, long-standing regional rivalries and anti-British sentiment led Nasser to vilify Iraq's membership. In this framework, it was proving very difficult for Nasser and the United States to build a solid relationship. When Western countries spurned Nasser's request for arms, he turned to the Eastern bloc and signed an arms deal with Czechoslovakia. Shortly thereafter, he recognized Communist China. Much to the United States' chagrin, Moscow appeared to be gaining a major foothold in the Arab world.

The flashpoint that brought war about in 1956 was the Suez Canal. Feeling that Nasser needed to be taught a lesson, the US government announced in July that it would withdraw funding for a hydroelectric and irrigation project called the Aswan High Dam, a key part of Nasser's development agenda. Nasser responded in July by nationalizing the Suez Canal Company, thus sparking an international crisis. Britain was deeply alarmed by Nasser's efforts to undermine its position in the region and, working with France, conspired with Israel to topple Nasser in October. However, the agreed-upon Israeli invasion of the Sinai Peninsula, followed in early November by the landing of British and French forces in the Canal Zone, brought swift condemnation from the US government. President Eisenhower feared that such outdated imperial tactics on the part of US allies would only further benefit the Soviet Union's position in the Middle East and indeed the wider Third World. America then strongly pressured Britain and France to withdraw their troops.

For Israel, whose military victory was stunning, the political consequences of the 1956 Suez War were mixed. On the one hand, its collusion in an act resembling 19th-century gunboat diplomacy further deepened the resentment felt across the Arab world. On the other hand, the war resulted in a United Nations Emergency Force (UNEF) taking up strategic positions in the Sinai Peninsula. The UNEF was entrusted with both preventing Palestinian guerrillas from crossing into Israel and ensuring Israel's right of maritime passage through the Straits of Tiran. Israel would view any future attempt to close the Straits of Tiran, its main achievement of the 1956 war, as a *casus belli*.

For Nasser, the notorious failure of the Anglo-French-Israeli invasion became a massive political victory. He had faced down the threat of renewed foreign domination. As Nasser's popular support soared in Egypt, so too did his stock throughout the Arab world where his rhetorical promises to confront what he called 'the Zionist entity' resonated. Nasser's dominant position did not, however, last for long. The heroic stature invested in Egypt's president after 1956 became an impossible burden by 1967, when rhetoric turned dramatically to action, and Nasser led Arab countries into a humiliating defeat.

Given that the problems over borders and refugees remained untenable, yet another violent round of fighting seemed inevitable in the wake of 1956. In the decade following the Suez War, Nasser became increasingly embroiled in an Arab cold war that pitched his leadership of a republican, reformist-minded bloc of Arab states against the more conservative and even reactionary monarchies. One conspicuous example of the instability of the situation was the fact that he committed 70,000 troops to a civil war in Yemen, and thereby got bogged down fighting a proxy war against Saudi Arabia. A second example was the engagement of all countries in an alarming multi-sided arms race, whereby Arab countries competed against each other, as well as against Israel, while Israel armed itself against all of them.

Moreover, Nasser's prominence unleashed new dynamics which he struggled with difficulty to control. When Soviet intelligence in May 1967 reported that Israel was preparing to launch an invasion of Syria, Nasser felt that his credibility demanded his support for fellow Arab progressives. He sought to deploy along the Sinai border enough Egyptian forces to deter Israel, but was in no position to go to war with Israel. Nonetheless, tensions escalated dramatically with the removal of the UNEF forces that had been acting as a shield between the two parties. When Nasser's forces occupied the UNEF post at the Straits of Tiran, and closed the shipping lines to Israel, he crossed the red line: the Israeli government had made it clear that it would not tolerate such a blockade. The military balance at that time favoured Israel, and so on 5 June 1967 Israel's air force launched a surprise attack on air bases throughout Egypt. It achieved air supremacy within hours, and over the next six days Israel found itself in occupation of the entire Sinai Peninsula, the West Bank, and the Golan Heights in south-western Syria.

Conclusion

In the two decades up to the 1967 war, Palestinians overwhelmingly invested their future in the promises made by external forces. Various Arab regimes and ideological movements offered their support, but the greatest amount of faith was placed in Gamal Abd al-Nasser. The defeat of 1967 fundamentally transformed Arab politics and the Palestinians' position in it. But, as Roger Owen observes, the position of Palestinians in the Arab world was always a complex one, possessing the capacity both to unite Arabs and to divide them. The escalating tension between the new state of Israel and her Arab neighbours fed a powerful pan-Arab orientation in regional politics prior to 1967, but the driving force was always the struggle for political independence and economic development by the distinct Arab states. To be sure, the Palestinian cause offered useful opportunities for newly independent Arab regimes to bolster their own legitimacy. And yet, throughout the Arab world, the nation-building process itself necessitated the development of their own particular identities and the demarcation of a separate Palestinian one. As for the Palestinians' own quest for a state, it would have to begin anew after the 1967 war.

Israel's post-independence leaders benefited greatly from their prior experience in the *Yishuv* building administrative and military structures. Much more complicated was the task of trying to sort out what exactly it meant for a state to be both democratic and Jewish. Important tensions remained. One challenge was determining what rights its Arab citizens ought to enjoy, and resolving the evident contradiction between the notion of a Jewish state and of a democracy granting equal rights to all. A second important set of challenges was posed by the unresolved need to define the nature of its relationship to the land of Biblical Israel, the most significant parts of which did not come under its control until the 1967 war. For Israelis the 1967 war was both a defensive and an opportunistic conflict. Taking advantage of surprise and superior arms, Israel won a spectacular military victory that placed it in control of all of the land of mandate Palestine, including the West Bank, the Gaza Strip, and East Jerusalem. In the eyes of some Israelis, the war represented a miraculous liberation of Eretz Israel, the lands of Biblical antiquity. But uppermost in the minds of others was the question of how to rule over a rapidly growing Arab population of 1.5 million people.

Chapter 5
Occupation 1967–87

The armistice agreements that ended the fighting in 1949 in effect delineated the de facto partition of mandate Palestine. Known as the Green Line, the resultant boundary provided international recognition of the borders that separated Israel, the Jordanian-annexed West Bank, and the Egyptian-ruled Gaza Strip for twenty years, until the 1967 war again changed the shape of the Palestinian–Israeli conflict. Israel's defeat of Egypt, Syria, and Jordan in the span of six days in June 1967 had far-reaching, if mixed, implications. On the one hand, by quadrupling the amount of territory held by Israel (including, as shown in Illustration 10, the Sinai Peninsula, Golan Heights, West Bank, and Gaza), the 1967 war provided it with territorial assets that created new opportunities for bilateral negotiations and could potentially lead to a historic reconciliation with her Arab neighbours. On the other hand, the scale and speed of Israel's military victory introduced complacency to the idea of accommodation and territorial compromise. Most problematically, the sudden conquest of territory steeped in Biblical history sparked within Israel expansionist aims that would make the conflict much more difficult to resolve.

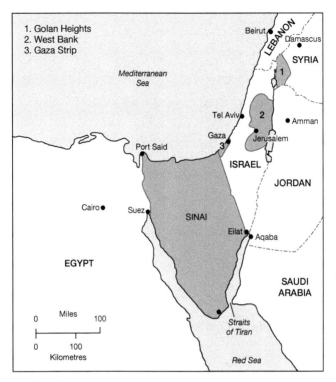

10. **The 1967 war**

UN Resolution 242 and the Israeli–Egyptian peace treaty

In the international arena, Israel's conquests were viewed as a bargaining chip with which it could leverage an end to the hostilities. The framework for such a deal was embodied in United Nations (UN) Security Council Resolution 242. Resolution 242, with its formula of a land-for-peace resolution to the conflict, became the basis for every subsequent attempt at peacemaking.

United Nations Security Council Resolution 242

22 November 1967

The Security Council,

Expressing its continuing concern with the grave situation in the Middle East,

Emphasizing the inadmissibility of the acquisition of territory by war and the need to work for a just and lasting peace in which every State in the area can live in security,

Emphasizing further that all Member States In thelr acceptance of the Charter of the United Nations have undertaken a commitment to act in accordance with Article 2 of the Charter,

1. *Affirms* that the fulfillment of Charter principles requires the establishment of a just and lasting peace in the Middle East which should include the application of both the following principles:

    (i) Withdrawal of Israel armed forces from territories occupied in the recent conflict;

    (ii) Termination of all claims or states of belligerency and respect for and acknowledgment of the sovereignty, territorial integrity and political independence of every State in the area and their right to live in peace within secure and recognized boundaries free from threats or acts of force;

2. *Affirms further* the necessity

    (a) For guaranteeing freedom of navigation through international waterways in the area;

    (b) For achieving a just settlement of the refugee problem;

    (Continued)

(c) For guaranteeing the territorial inviolability and political independence of every State in the area, through measures including the establishment of demilitarized zones;

3. *Requests* the Secretary-General to designate a Special Representative to proceed to the Middle East to establish and maintain contacts with the States concerned in order to promote agreement and assist efforts to achieve a peaceful and accepted settlement in accordance with the provisions and principles in this resolution . . .

Israel, Egypt, Jordan, and Lebanon accepted the resolution (Syria waited until 1973, the Palestinians until 1988). But they based their acceptance on divergent interpretations. Whereas the Arab states called for Israel to withdraw from *all* of the occupied land, Israel argued the case that the omission of the definite article—*the* territories—implied by omission that it could hold on to some occupied territory. Not surprisingly, such ambiguity engendered diplomatic deadlock. Meanwhile Arab leaders met in Khartoum, the capital of Sudan. The conference, held at the end of August 1967, resulted in the famous 'three noes': no recognition, no negotiation, and no peace with Israel. The defiance expressed by the Arab summit certainly complicated the process of building on the framework put forth by Resolution 242. But the stance taken at Khartoum did leave open the prospect of a peaceful settlement, if not a peace treaty, if the superpowers would undertake to act as third-party mediators. Indeed, for both Egyptian President Gamal Abd al-Nasser and Jordan's King Husayn, their acceptance of Resolution 242 signalled informal acceptance of Israel. With neither the Soviet Union nor the United States showing the capacity or will to enforce the UN resolution, the failure to implement 242 can be attributed also to the basic asymmetry in the negotiating positions of the various parties. Israel, with its by now overwhelming military superiority, was in no hurry to initiate talks. For their part, Arab countries were not prepared to negotiate from a position of weakness. Progress on the land-for-peace formula would have to wait for radical changes to the geopolitical situation.

In the years following the 1967 war, relations between Egypt and Israel steadily deteriorated amidst a series of artillery exchanges. In March 1969 Egypt launched a low-intensity 'war of attrition' aimed at breaking the diplomatic impasse and preventing the 1967 ceasefire line along the Suez Canal from hardening into a de facto border. The aim of the Egyptian attacks was to wear down the Israeli fortifications and raise the economic costs of the Sinai occupation, but Egypt suffered more from Israeli reprisals. By the time Nasser agreed to a ceasefire in August 1970, shortly before his death, the region's political impasse had brought about significant alignments with the superpowers. The Soviet Union resupplied the Egyptian military, while the United States saw Israel as a useful ally against perceived Soviet advances.

What finally broke the diplomatic stalemate was a coordinated surprise attack by Egypt and Syria in October 1973. When Anwar Sadat succeeded Nasser as president of Egypt in 1970, he inherited a very difficult set of economic and diplomatic problems. Sadat had tried to encourage US participation in lessening the tensions, breaking his country's military ties with the Soviet Union, but found he still had no leverage with which to bring it about. Reaching the conclusion that only a limited war could improve Egypt's negotiating position, Sadat launched an attack on Israeli forces occupying the Sinai Peninsula. He hoped to create an international crisis that would force US engagement in a negotiating process. The Egyptian attack was secretly coordinated with a Syrian attack on the occupied Golan Heights. During the war, Saudi Arabia proclaimed an oil embargo directed at any nation (above all, the United States) that supported Israel's military efforts. Israeli counter-attacks effectively reversed the early momentum of the Syrian and Egyptian armies, but tensions between the two superpowers were indeed raised to a level that demanded their diplomatic intervention.

Accordingly, even though Egypt's military results were mixed, the war successfully engineered the new bargaining environment sought by Sadat. The Egyptian army had performed admirably; the myth of Israeli invincibility had been broken, and for the first time a settlement to the Arab–Israeli conflict had become a top priority concern for the United States. The new diplomatic effort first took the form of negotiating small disengagement agreements between Israel and her neighbours. In the years following the 1973 war, US Secretary of State and National Security Adviser Henry Kissinger embarked upon several rounds of 'shuttle diplomacy' aimed at moving, step by step, towards a political settlement. In the short term at least, these agreements benefited both Israel and Egypt: Israel received further assurance of US diplomatic and financial support and Egypt saw the return of some territory, including restoration of the canal and important oilfields.

However, Israel remained in control of most of the Sinai Peninsula. Disappointed with the hesitant progress of international efforts, Anwar Sadat visited Israel in November 1977. It was a dramatic initiative, aimed at dismantling the psychological barriers that had solidified since the Khartoum conference. Its main effect, though, was to prioritize Egypt's own interests, as distinct from Arab interests or those of the Palestinians. The visit led in 1978 to a separate Israeli–Egyptian peace mediated by President Jimmy Carter at the presidential retreat at Camp David. At the outset, Carter envisaged using Resolution 242 as a framework for negotiating a general peace, including the withdrawal of Israeli forces from the West Bank and Gaza in return for Palestinian recognition of Israel's right to secure and recognized boundaries. In fact, the Camp David accords stipulated transitional arrangements for the West Bank and Gaza that would lead to 'full autonomy' for its inhabitants. But the accords, formally signed in March 1979, succeeded only in applying the land-for-peace formula to a normalization of diplomatic relations between Egypt and Israel. Sadat was so desperate to get the Sinai back that he simply resigned himself to signing a separate peace. As for the newly elected Israeli Prime Minister, Menachem Begin, his right-wing Likud Party refused outright to commit to any recognition of Palestinian self-determination in the West Bank and Gaza, territory Begin referred to only by its Biblical name of Judea and Samaria. Under Begin's leadership, the Palestinian territories were considered an inalienable part of the Jewish people's Biblical inheritance. And with Egypt now alienated from the rest of the Arab world, Begin could try to impose his own circumscribed notion of what a settlement with the Palestinians would look like. In the meantime, he sped up the construction of Jewish settlements in their midst.

Israel and the settlements

Israel's conquest in 1967 of the West Bank, or 'Judea and Samaria' as Israel referred to it, marked a fundamental turning point in the evolution of Zionism. The 1947 UN plan and the 1949 armistice lines had provided Zionism with territory in which to achieve its political goals—the main one being statehood. But these borders had not included the ancient lands of Israel. Throughout, and prior to, the mandate period, Jewish settlement had been attracted mostly to the economic opportunities offered by the plains and valleys of mandate Palestine. The religious sites of the central mountainous range remained densely populated by the indigenous Arab population and so were not included in the UN plans for a Jewish state. As David Ben Gurion argued at the first meeting of the Israeli Knesset, a Jewish state that incorporated the West Bank could not be democratic because of its large Arab population. However, other Zionist leaders never accepted the 1947 partition, while others viewed it solely in terms of a stepping stone for further expansion. Those who perceived the conquests of 1967 as the final restoration of the lands of Israel, and portrayed their cause as the fulfilment of Jewish destiny, were bolstered by the support of hard-line leaders, often referred to as 'hawks', who argued after 1967 for the incorporation of the West Bank and Gaza into the Jewish state for security reasons. They asserted, for example, that the Jordan Valley was Israel's only defensible border. In this highly charged debate over Israel's boundaries, the hawks were opposed by the 'doves', who continued to place more emphasis on implementing a land-for-peace deal envisaged by Resolution 242. They supported, for example, a territorial negotiation with King Husayn of Jordan. This conflict was also taken up by extra-parliamentary movements such as Peace Now and Gush Emunim (Bloc of the Faithful). Whereas Peace Now emerged as a secular movement that supported territorial compromise, Gush Emunim was a religious millenarian movement whose goal was to secure an indissoluble degree of Israeli control over the occupied territories. It saw its task as one of establishing irreversible facts on the ground that would make future negotiations difficult if not impossible. Accordingly, the movement founded new Jewish settlements deep in the West Bank, both on relatively uninhabited hilltops and in dense population centres.

In the years immediately following the 1967 war, those agitating for withdrawal and negotiation were very much on the defensive. They found it especially difficult to press their case: Israel's geopolitical position seemed invincible, and the belligerence shown by Arab leaders at Khartoum hardened the case against any compromise. It was an environment in which the messianic nationalist vision could only grow stronger. The transformation in attitudes towards the need to assert Biblical rights was sharpest in the case of Arab cities such as Hebron—where a few hundred Jewish settlers needed to be protected by at least as many soldiers—and Jerusalem. Before 1967, Zionist leaders could imagine a Jewish state without Jerusalem. After 1967, Israelis agreed unanimously on the need to control the whole city. As shown in Illustration 11, the Green Line which had separated Jordanian East Jerusalem from Israeli West Jerusalem was discarded and the jurisdiction of the Israeli municipality was

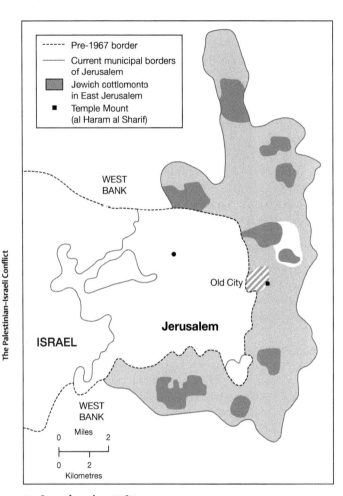

Pre-1967 border

Current municipal borders
of Jerusalem

Jewish settlements
in East Jerusalem

Temple Mount
(al Haram al Sharif)

WEST
BANK

ISRAEL

Jerusalem

Old City

WEST
BANK

Miles
0   2

0   2
Kilometres

11. Jerusalem since 1967

extended to include East Jerusalem. Within the old city, the
medieval Mughrabi quarter was demolished to make room for an
open space in front of the Western Wall; on the outskirts,
municipal boundaries were expanded in order to extend Israeli

jurisdiction over the lands of neighbouring Arab villages. A systematic settlement policy resulted in the construction of a ring of Jewish suburbs encircling Jerusalem. Yet, although a 1980 Knesset resolution declared Jerusalem the eternal capital of Israel, the peoples of East and West Jerusalem enjoyed little contact. Israel's annexation was not recognized by the international community and Palestinians themselves saw East Jerusalem as the future capital of their own independent state.

With gradual, if at first hesitant, acquiescence from the government, and spurred by increasing support of a public nostalgia for the ethic and operations of early Zionist pioneers, thousands of Israelis established mobile home settlements in the West Bank and Gaza during the decade after 1967. The Labour-led government in Israel at the time voiced support for the exchange of land for peace but nonetheless invested significantly in settlement infrastructure in the occupied territories. Settlement activity increased dramatically after the 1977 elections and the Likud victory over the Labour Party. After decades of political pre-eminence, Labour Zionism's electoral defeat was in large part attributed to its failure to provide a clear ideological response to the question of the legitimacy of the settlement project. The growing disenchantment with the Labour Party can also be attributed to the emerging political involvement of the Mizrahi population, which felt increasingly alienated by the policies of the Labour Party's Ashkenazi elite. Mizrahi groups formed the backbone of support for the victory of Menachem Begin and the Likud Party in the 1977 elections. Begin was committed to increased settlement building as a way to ensure that future governments would be forced to retain control over the territories, and he introduced a number of government subsidies that would broaden the territories' appeal beyond the religious settler movement. Many settlements built along the Green Line were designed to appeal to commuters from Tel Aviv and West Jerusalem. For Begin, Israel's signing of the 1979 peace accords with Egypt was both the beginning and the end of a land-for-peace accord.

Whether settlements were established for reasons of conviction or convenience, they were all heavily protected by a military occupation that imposed heavy burdens on the Palestinian inhabitants. Israel severely restricted economic life in the occupied territories: for example, agricultural land was expropriated for Israeli settlements and military installations and irrigation farming suffered from the refusal of army officers to permit the digging of wells. Meanwhile, subsidized Israeli agricultural products were sold widely in the occupied territories. The Palestinian economy became increasingly subject and subordinate to the needs of the growing Israeli economy. Palestinian farm labourers left home to work in Israel or even found work constructing Jewish settlements, while those with the appropriate skills sought employment in the oil-rich Gulf countries.

Palestinians

As noted above, the fighting that ended in 1949 erased Palestine from the map and destroyed Palestinian society. Over 700,000 Palestinians became refugees. Barred from returning to their villages, most of which were soon bulldozed by Israel, Palestinian refugees were dispersed among surrounding Arab countries, with a high proportion going to the West Bank and Gaza. However, new form was given to Palestinian nationalist identity by their common insistence on their right to return. The United Nations Relief and Works Agency (UNRWA) played an important role in providing services, especially in education. Set up in 1949 to provide relief services, UNRWA gradually took on more responsibility in the fields of education and health. But the fact that the refugees' livelihood was basically dependent upon the goodwill of distinct host states resulted also in Palestinian political and social fragmentation. For example, in Lebanon—where some 150,000 Palestinian refugees threatened to upset the delicate population balance on which the governmental system of proportional communal representation was based—more Palestinian Christians were absorbed into Lebanese society than

Palestinian Muslims. Proportionately, the Gaza Strip admitted the largest number of refugees: its 80,000 inhabitants, who in 1948 came under Egypt's military administration, absorbed 200,000 refugees. Only Jordan conferred citizenship upon the refugees: for King Abdullah, gaining control over the important Muslim shrines of Jerusalem's Old City and bolstering his regional importance fully justified the annexation of the newly carved-out West Bank, refugee camps and all. West Bank resources and manpower tended to promote the development of the East Bank.

In 1964, the creation of the Palestinian Liberation Organization (PLO) gave Palestinians a new focus of political identity. Its charter called for a Palestinian Arab state on all the whole of mandate Palestine, describing it as an 'indivisible territorial unit' and declaring the establishment of Israel 'illegal and null and void'. When the PLO was formed at the first Arab summit, many prominent Palestinians participated but they became highly suspicious of the organization's evident subordination to Egyptian President Nasser. The organization's effectiveness as a national institution was further curtailed by the opposition of Jordan's King Husayn, who viewed it as a threat to his claim of sovereignty over the West Bank and its inhabitants. Meanwhile, other Palestinian groups were also organizing themselves with the aim of taking control of their own struggle against Israel. The most important of these groups was Fatah (Arabic for 'conquest'), founded in Kuwait in 1959 and led by Yasir Arafat.

Arafat's ability to move the PLO beyond the tutelage of Arab states and take control of the organization as a whole came as a direct result of their defeat in June 1967. The war seriously weakened the hold of Arab states on Palestinian activity, and hurt the legitimacy of the previous PLO leadership. In March 1968, Fatah launched guerrilla operations against the West Bank from bases in Jordanian villages. After an Israeli reprisal attack on the village of Karamah met fierce resistance by the guerrillas, who were supported by the Jordanian army, the battle of Karamah (the name means 'honour' or 'dignity' in Arabic) became a symbol of heroic resistance. Fatah's popularity then soared, inspiring a rapid influx of volunteers, donations, and armaments. Wearing his black-and-white chequered *keffiyeh* (head cloth), Arafat became the public face of the Palestinian guerrilla movement. In 1969 he was elected chairman of the PLO (a position he held until his death in 2004). In 1974, at the Arab summit held in Rabat, the PLO received recognition as the sole representative of the Palestinians. And later that year, Arafat addressed the UN general assembly and the PLO was granted observer status.

Adopting the tone of contemporary radical anti-colonial movements, the 1968 Palestine Charter placed special emphasis on armed struggle as a strategy and not just a tactic and thus as the only way to bring about the liberation of Palestine. It rejected Zionism's claims on any part of Palestine, acknowledging Judaism only as a religion, not a nationality. The organization's embrace of armed struggle contributed to mobilizing Palestinians and attracted international attention to their plight. But the PLO was an umbrella organization and Fatah's role, though dominant, was not uncontested. Given Palestinian dispersal, Arafat preferred to try to bring all factions, some of which had very different agendas, under a big tent rather than place a premium on discipline and obedience. His persistent failure to oppose the more violent approaches embraced by smaller militant groups (such as the terrorist operation against Israeli athletes at the Munich Olympics in 1972 and the 1985 hijacking of an Italian passenger ship, the *Achille Lauro*, during which a Jewish American tourist was murdered) tended to undermine the legitimacy of the Palestinian movement and solidify the image of Palestinians as terrorists on the world stage. It also brought the organization into conflict with neighbouring host countries such as Jordan and Lebanon. The relationship between Arab governments and Palestinian nationalism was an ever-shifting one: generally, the regimes' rhetoric espousing the liberation of Palestine was backed up by limited support or a desire to control the movement for their own purposes.

In particular, the relationship between the PLO and Jordan, where Palestinians established bases from which to organize guerrilla armed struggle against Israel, was volatile from the outset. It ended in disaster in 1970 when the Popular Front for the Liberation of Palestine (PFLP), a component of the PLO which was determined to overthrow the Hashemite monarchy, staged multiple hijackings of international airline flights. King Husayn declared war on the PLO after accusing it of creating 'a state within a state', and killed 3,000 Palestinians in the process. Expelled from Jordan, most PLO guerrillas regrouped in Lebanon, where Arafat soon established a number of social and economic organizations and indeed relocated the entire PLO infrastructure there.

But its presence in Lebanon increasingly threatened the country's delicate political and demographic balance. When civil war broke out in 1975, Lebanon's Christian leaders were particularly concerned about the challenge the Palestinian 'state within a state' posed to their political dominance. They sought help from Israeli leaders who were equally concerned about the presence of PLO guerrillas on their northern border. In 1982, an assassination attempt on Israel's ambassador to the United Kingdom provided the Israeli government with a pretext to invade Lebanon and expel the PLO from its power base in Beirut. In June, Israeli troops pushed up the coastline. They moved deep into Lebanon, occupying the south and then laying siege to the capital. As Beirut came under heavy bombardment, the PLO faced pressure from most Lebanese political parties to leave. In August thousands of Palestinian fighters were forced to evacuate, and the PLO leadership along with many fighters withdrew to Tunisia, Syria, and further afield. The following month, Lebanese Christian militiamen entered the now unarmed Palestinian refugee camps of Sabra and Shatila and, with the help of the protective presence and night-time flares provided by the surrounding Israeli army, slaughtered thousands, including women and children.

The costs of the war for Lebanon were staggering, and the regional repercussions of Israel's invasion of Lebanon were also profound. Politically, an important new force emerged in south Lebanon. The predominantly Shi'ite Muslim community had initially welcomed an end to PLO armed operations, which had made the area a dangerous place in which to live. But Shi'ite resentment of Israel intensified as an Israeli occupation in the south took root. Israel had hoped that the expansion of a 'security zone' stretching 5 to 25 kilometres inside Lebanon would offer Israel a protective buffer. Instead, it quickly replaced one foe with another. On Israel's northern frontier, the fight against occupation was now led by the newly established Shi'ite militias Amal and, later, Hizbullah (Party of God). In the struggle for control over their land, Amal and Hizbullah launched violent guerrilla campaigns assisted by Syria and Iran. Israel finally withdrew fifteen years later.

Reverberations of the Lebanon war were also strongly felt in Israel's domestic politics. The invasion left Israelis deeply divided. As news of the atrocities dominated the headlines, protests against Israel's role in the Lebanon war mounted, and Prime Minister Menachem Begin faced increasing pressure to form a commission of inquiry to investigate the Sabra and Shatila massacre. The commission called for the dismissal of Defence Minister Ariel Sharon, while public pressure increased on Begin to resign, which he did the following year.

For Palestinians, the fallout from the Lebanon war was also profound. In exile in Tunisia, the PLO leadership now looked out upon a very different political landscape. With very little to show for eighteen years of armed struggle, the focus gradually shifted to the pursuit of diplomatic initiatives. A new strategy developed, involving recognition of the existence of the Israeli state and envisaging a redefinition of a state of Palestine based on the West Bank and Gaza, and not on the whole of the post-First World War mandate territory. However, shifts in international relations at this time, in particular the end of the Cold War, threatened to lessen dramatically the PLO's significance as well as its cause. Confined to Tunis, the PLO's central leadership drifted, until thrown a lifeline by the 1987 uprising against the Israeli occupation, known as the *intifada*.

Conclusion

The 1967 Arab–Israeli war opened new possibilities for a settlement to the ongoing conflict. In control of major territorial assets, Israel now had something to trade for peace with neighbouring states. However, at the same time as Israel increased its leverage in negotiations, powerful interests emerged within it that militated against a return of the occupied territories and favoured an expanded 'Greater Israel'. Control over the West Bank and Gaza fuelled the messianic belief that war had fulfilled Jewish destiny. Jewish settlers mobilized support by drawing upon a certain nostalgia for early Zionist settlement work. This time, however, the pioneers were implementing the Zionist dream in the hills of Judea and Samaria. Settlements were strategically located to deliberately thwart any effort to implement the land-for-peace model mandated by Resolution 242. They thus reopened the problematic question of where exactly Israel's borders lay, and a new challenge emerged: how to maintain a democratic Jewish state while also annexing a large and growing Arab population.

By 1987, the Palestinian population of the West Bank and Gaza had spent twenty years under an unbearable occupation. With their Tunisian central leadership powerless, a younger generation took matters into their own hands. The spark was a road accident at the main junction between Israel and the Gaza Strip that caused four Palestinian deaths. Their funerals ignited protests, and within days the occupied territories were engulfed in demonstrations that mobilized all Palestinians, including women and children. Both the Israeli and the PLO leaderships were surprised by the spontaneous uprising, and both had to craft their responses quickly. Israel resorted to brute force, but this only fuelled more resistance. Enervated by the inability of Israel's military might to quell the disturbances, increasing numbers of Israelis turned against the occupation and what they saw as its corrupting impact. The PLO leaders, on the other hand, felt empowered by the grass-roots rebellion and confidently sought to translate the momentum of the resistance into diplomatic achievement. In 1988, the PLO affirmed Resolution 242, recognized the Israeli state, and called for a peaceful settlement between Israel and a Palestinian state located in the West Bank and Gaza Strip. It would be another defining moment in the evolution of the Palestinian–Israeli conflict.

Chapter 6
The rise and fall of the peace process 1987–2007

Following the failure of diplomatic efforts in the wake of the 1982 Lebanon war, the 1987 Palestinian *intifada* (which means 'shaking off' in Arabic) carried the conflict back into the spotlight of the international arena. Television images of Palestinian youths armed with slingshots facing off against Israeli tanks upended common international perceptions of a David and Goliath conflict. The *intifada* also fundamentally transformed political equations on the ground. More than a venting of anger at the Israeli occupation, the *intifada* was a powerful expression of the depth of Palestinian nationalism.

As the *intifada* gathered steam in the late 1980s, the PLO and the Israeli government were both forced to devise appropriate responses. Both had been taken by surprise by the scope and nature of the *intifada*. The *intifada* forced and empowered the Arafat leadership in Tunis to develop new diplomatic strategies based on a two-state solution. Eager to capitalize on the political momentum to gain international legitimacy, the PLO in 1988 accepted Resolution 242 and recognized Israel's right to exist. Israel too was forced to respond to the transformed landscape. Searching for ways to disengage from the direct violence of the *intifada*, which was increasingly spearheaded by the militant religious group, Hamas, Israel initiated direct talks in 1993 with PLO leaders. After reaching an agreement in secret talks in Oslo, Norway, Israeli and

Palestinian dignitaries were invited by US President Bill Clinton to sign the new accords on the White House Lawn. At the time, the event was considered a groundbreaking moment.

From *intifada* to peace process

PLO leaders living in exile in Tunisia worried about becoming increasingly marginalized. Inside the West Bank and Gaza, the protests comprised all strata of Palestinian society and gave birth to a new, young, and clandestine leadership known as the Unified National Leadership of the Uprising (UNLU). Though composed of representatives of the main PLO factions, this local leadership encouraged grass-roots initiatives aimed at making the occupation an immoral and unaffordable burden on Israeli society. Popular committees were mobilized to coordinate acts of civil disobedience, including the boycotting of Israeli goods and services and replacing them with those produced through local networks, and to organize daily life with the eventual aim of achieving self-determination. With the political initiative lying firmly in the hands of Palestinian leaders inside the occupied territories, a certain tension emerged between the local leadership and the outside PLO. But the successful coordination of the political goals of the UNLU with those of the PLO provided salvation to its chairman, Yasir Arafat, and his fellow Fatah colleagues. Further validation of Arafat's role came in July 1988 when King Husayn dropped Jordan's claims to the West Bank.

However, the *intifada* also gave birth to a religious resistance movement that outright challenged the PLO's authority. Best known by the acronym Hamas (*Harakat al-Muqawama al-Islamiyya*, or Islamic Resistance Movement), which means 'zeal' in Arabic, this movement was an offshoot of the Gaza branch of the Muslim Brotherhood. The Muslim Brotherhood had long been involved in religious missionary activities. When the *intifada* erupted, younger, university-educated leaders in the movement feared that it would lose support if it did not get involved politically. Initially encouraged by the Israeli government as a counterweight to the PLO, Hamas built on its long record of providing social services in the occupied territories and gained widespread popularity during the *intifada*. It vehemently opposed the PLO's willingness to compromise on the partition of historic Palestine. Hamas's platform sacralized the whole of what had been mandate Palestine, calling for the destruction of Israel and the establishment of a 'state of Islam'. Crude and simplistic as its initial charter was, the movement's popularity, and its ability to mobilize an effective network of institutions, posed a real challenge to Fatah's authority.

For Israel, the impact of this rapidly changing political landscape was profound. Israel's eventual success in arresting many of the UNLU leaders led to the gradual disintegration of the grass-roots networks, but not before their civil disobedience campaigns had effectively convinced many Israelis that the occupied territories could no longer be considered a secure economic or even defensive asset. The Israeli state's initial decision to use the brutal force of an 'iron fist' to crush the *intifada* had only fuelled further rebellion while tarnishing the state's reputation abroad as well as at home. Israelis became convinced that the status quo was both morally and practically untenable, and increasing numbers began to pressure their government to extricate itself from the occupied territories.

A further push towards some kind of political reconciliation was spurred on by Iraq's 1990 invasion and occupation of Kuwait. US forces, supported by a multilateral coalition that included many Arab countries, had little difficulty dislodging Iraq's forces from Kuwait. During the war itself, however, Iraq launched scud missiles against Israeli cities, hoping to break up the coalition. These missiles, which Israel feared were equipped with chemical warheads, exposed Israelis to new threats and vulnerabilities, against which control over the West Bank and Gaza offered little defence. Furthermore, the war against Iraq's occupation of Kuwait generated growing calls that the United States also bring an end to the Israeli occupation of Palestinians. Indeed, following its 1991 victory in the Gulf War, the United States moved quickly to convene an international peace conference in Madrid in which all the states of the region participated (without the PLO). The Gulf War had in fact greatly weakened the position of the PLO. Arafat's decision to side with Iraq dictator Saddam Husayn left him isolated diplomatically and financially cut off from further contributions from oil-rich Gulf countries: the PLO lost subsidies that it had previously received from the Kuwaiti and Saudi governments, and over 300,000 Palestinians resident in Kuwait lost their homes and their livelihoods. Israel effectively barred PLO officials from attending the Madrid conference but negotiators from the West Bank and Gaza nonetheless participated under the PLO's authority. They gave by far the most eloquent speeches. Not only were Palestinian demands framed in reasonable terms, they were presented face to face to Israeli leaders for the first time. The Madrid talks otherwise achieved little of substance beyond securing a commitment from all parties to support an ongoing framework of bilateral negotiations. With the exception of the Israel–Jordan talks, which led successfully in 1994 to a peace treaty, the bilateral negotiations soon became stalemated. In these post-Madrid meetings, the main sticking point was Israeli settlement policies. The Palestinian delegation led by the 'insiders'—leaders who lived and worked in the occupied territories—insisted on a settlement freeze.

The *intifada*'s operations against the Israeli occupation continued after Madrid. Yet they seemed to become more fragmented, more militarized, and increasingly overshadowed by internecine fighting. Then suddenly, in late August 1993, it was disclosed that a small team of individuals representing the PLO and the Israeli government had reached an agreement, while meeting in complete secrecy in Oslo, Norway. The whole world—including Palestinian and Israeli delegates in Washington who were gearing up for yet another round of Madrid talks—was astonished.

The rise and fall of the Oslo accords

The 1993 Oslo accords did not emerge from a vacuum. Their centrepiece was an agreement formally known as the Declaration of Principles on Palestinian Self-Rule (DOP), which sketched out a phased approach to Palestinian autonomy that was consistent with the timetable outlined by the 1979 Camp David talks. The main difference was that Oslo provided for formal mutual recognition between the PLO and Israel. The PLO renounced the use of violence and recognized Israel's right to peace and security and, in return, Israel recognized the PLO as the representative of the Palestinian people. The first phase of the Oslo process consisted of a transitional period, not meant to exceed five years, during which a newly elected government, known as the Palestinian Authority, would be given a territorial base from which to begin the process of self-governance.

The basic assumption of the Oslo process was that new partnerships would form as Israelis and Palestinians together developed administrative and security arrangements. Step by small step, the interim period was expected to build the trust and momentum necessary for the eventual discussion of the thorniest issues, which were placed in the short term on the back-burner. Known as the 'final status issues', these were the most difficult and complex—the borders and status of a Palestinian state, the claims and repatriation of the Palestinian refugees, the fate of the Jewish settlements, and the disposition of East Jerusalem. The Oslo process said nothing about these issues. Oslo was not about forging a permanent peace agreement based on Resolution 242: it was all about building the political space that would allow for a later negotiation.

Whether or not the phased two-stage approach represented a necessary, or even genuine, move towards a final resolution to the conflict, it was essential that the interim agreements be implemented promptly and in good faith. For political momentum to have a chance to build, Palestinians and Israelis at the grass-roots level needed to see immediate benefits of the compromises being made by their leaders. Delay in the Oslo process thus only worked to the benefit of the extremists on both sides who sought to destroy it.

For Palestinians, the misery of occupation in fact worsened under the Oslo framework. A major contributor to this was the continued expansion of the whole infrastructure of Jewish settlements in the occupied territories. The number of Israeli Jews living in the occupied territories rose dramatically, from approximately 250,000 in 1993 to almost 400,000 in 2003. So did the confiscation of land that was required to construct an elaborate system of bypass roads connecting the settlements but fragmenting Palestinian society. The five-year transition period envisaged by Oslo was specified in the 1995 Oslo II agreement, which divided the Palestinian territory into three zones—'A', 'B', and 'C' (see Illustration 12)—while calling for a phased redeployment of the Israeli military. Most of the Palestinian population resided in zones 'A' (the major towns) and 'B' (the major village areas), which came to form a patchwork of dozens of separate districts. Area 'C', almost three-quarters of the territory, was to remain under Israeli control. It contained the Israeli settlements and was the only contiguous area. In combination with Israel's continued control of the water supply, the restrictions that these divisions placed on the Palestinian economy resulted in increasing unemployment and poverty. Israel's actions during this period made Oslo look to many Palestinians like a trap, reminiscent of the South African Bantustans.

Palestinians' deepening frustration with Oslo stemmed also from the perceived failures of the accords' architect, Arafat, as a government leader. His desire to replicate in the West Bank and Gaza the decision-making processes developed in exile, and to centralize and monopolize the power hierarchy in the new Palestinian Authority faced strong opposition from two poles of

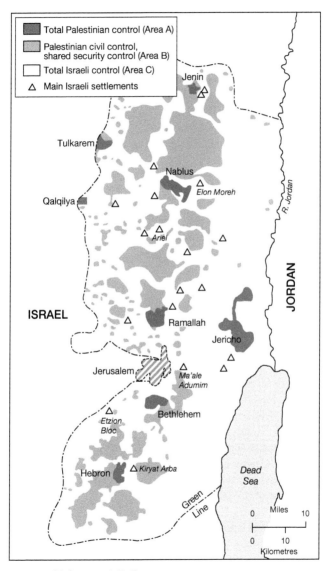

The legend reads:

- Total Palestinian control (Area A)
- Palestinian civil control, shared security control (Area B)
- Total Israeli control (Area C)
- △ Main Israeli settlements

Jenin

Tulkarem

Nablus

Elon Moreh

Qalqilya

Ariel

ISRAEL

Ramallah

Jericho

Jerusalem

Ma'ale Adumim

Bethlehem

Etzion Bloc

Hebron △ *Kiryat Arba*

JORDAN

R. Jordan

Dead Sea

Green Line

Miles
0 — 10

0 — 10
Kilometres

The rise and fall of the peace process 1987–2007

12. Map of Oslo areas A, B, C

local leadership. One was the younger leadership resident in the West Bank and Gaza who had gained experience from the popular committees that had sustained the *intifada* but now found themselves undermined by the new Palestinian Authority. Pivotal as they were in elevating Fatah exiles to proto-state politics in the form of the new Palestinian Authority, this younger leadership was perceived as a threat to Arafat and his old-guard coterie, who were increasingly referred to as 'the Tunisians'. A second group of local leaders also born of the *intifada* and who resented Arafat unfairly reaping the benefits of their resistance work was Hamas. In rejecting Fatah's idea of a negotiated partition, and by referring to all of mandate Palestine, including present-day Israel, as an Islamic *waqf* (religious trust), Hamas for many years rejected anything to do with the Oslo accords. By positioning itself as the main opposition to Fatah, Hamas then became the chief beneficiary to the growing disillusionment with the cronyism of Arafat's authority. Furthermore, fearing marginalization if Oslo actually succeeded, Hamas had a vested interest in ensuring its failure. From 1994, its sabotage of the Oslo process took the form of suicide bombings against civilian targets in Israel.

For many Israelis, the whole point of the Oslo accords was to secure the Palestinians' commitment to end armed violence and to resolve the conflict peacefully. 'Enough of blood and tears, enough,' announced Prime Minister Rabin on the White House Lawn in 1993, to which Arafat responded by assuring Israelis that Palestinian sovereignty was Israel's strongest guarantee of its security. But Arafat's failure to curb Hamas's violence against Israeli civilians profoundly increased their suspicions of the Palestinian leadership, and raised deeply felt fears over the emergence of an independent Palestinian state.

Emotions ran highest among militant Israeli groups, who, mirroring Hamas, framed their opposition to the Oslo process in religious terms. For them Oslo was more than a security risk; it was an abandonment of God's mandate. In 1995, one young religious extremist, Yigal Amir, assassinated Prime Minister Rabin during a massive peace rally in Tel Aviv. Amir had concluded that Rabin's death was sanctioned by the Prime Minister's willingness to forfeit tracts of land intended by God exclusively for the Jews. In 1996 elections, the Likud leader Benjamin Netanyahu was elected prime minister by a narrow margin. During the campaign, held during a surge of suicide bombings undertaken by Hamas, Netanyahu presented himself as 'Mr Security' and ran on a platform of slowing down the peace process. He had opposed the Oslo accords, not willing to give up control over the West Bank, what he referred to as Judea and Samaria, and refusing to acknowledge any connection between land and peace. Upon becoming prime minister, Netanyahu announced that the Israeli military would make no further redeployments in the West Bank and Gaza until Arafat complied scrupulously with all of the security provisions. His goal was for Israel alone to determine the location and extent of any future redeployments, while continuing to build settlements in the territory it controlled.

A volatile period, Netanyahu's first term as prime minister (1996–9) witnessed the derailing of the Oslo accords. The military control and closures exercised by the Israeli Defence Forces in Area C worsened an already dire economic situation throughout the occupied territories. Netanyahu's demand that Arafat crack down on Hamas reduced the Palestinian leader in the eyes of most of his people to the role of Israel's policeman. Given the basic power imbalance between the two sides, Arafat had little leverage with which to prevent Netanyahu from slowing down or reversing the Oslo process. A desperate attempt to restore momentum was made by the United States at the Wye Summit held in September 1998. Netanyahu agreed to further gradual redeployments of the Israeli military from Zones B and C, and in return Arafat committed Palestinian forces to cooperate closely with the Central Intelligence Agency in curbing Hamas activity. But Netanyahu's concessions lost him the support of his own political base. The coalition of religious and nationalist parties on which Netanyahu depended was already riddled by dissension, and his government was brought down before he could follow through on the promised redeployments. With the five-year interim period of the Oslo accords coming to a close, the all-important discussion of the contentious issues that had been left for the final status talks (sovereignty, refugees, settlements, Jerusalem) had yet to be broached.

Camp David II and the al-Aqsa *intifada*

Whatever the initial promise of Oslo, negotiations on the final status issues had to await the last-ditch efforts of Labour leader Ehud Barak, elected prime minister in 1999. These negotiations took place during a momentous round of diplomacy convened by President Clinton in 2000 at the same presidential retreat where President Carter had mediated the historic deal between Begin and Sadat. In what came to be known as Camp David II, Clinton, Arafat, and Barak spent a couple of weeks in July 2000 trying to end over a century of conflict. Going in with little advance preparation, and substantial gaps separating the stated positions on the thorniest issues, the summit by all accounts faced the odds of a 'Hail Mary Pass', a final, desperate attempt to score at the end of the game. Not only did the Israeli and Palestinian leaders face huge challenges in bridging the chasm between them, they also had to navigate the growing gulf that separated them from large segments of their populations at home. Neither leader had made much effort to prepare their people for the agonizing compromises that would be needed to achieve a historic reconciliation in the final status negotiations.

The two-week conference ended in anger and frustration. Amidst competing attempts to allocate blame, both sides came out more distrustful than ever about the real intentions of the other. Because no written offers were minuted during the conference, reports on the precise nature of the exchanges between the two negotiating teams differ widely. Barak is reported to have offered proposals—on the sharing of Jerusalem as well as on the percentage of West Bank territory on which a future Palestinian state could be built—that went far beyond what previous Israeli negotiators had countenanced. Nonetheless, the package fell well short of Palestinian demands, especially regarding the question of sovereignty over Jerusalem and recognition of the rights of Palestinian refugees. Israeli negotiators were angered by the unwillingness of the Palestinian side to respond with counterproposals, and accused them of not bargaining in good faith. For their part, Palestinians were deeply suspicious from the outset that the United States and Israel were colluding against them. Moreover, they were vexed by Barak's arrogant negotiating style and greatly resented the notion that occupied territories were being 'offered' to them, as opposed to 'returned'.

Unbridgeable as the gaps remained during the initial Camp David II summit, they did narrow, and enough had been achieved to warrant the continuation of talks by individual Palestinian and Israeli negotiators. At the end of September, Barak and Arafat again met cordially. More significantly, in December, and on the verge of leaving office, President Clinton put in one last effort as mediator by drawing up his own set of parameters for a peace settlement. According to Clinton's plan, the Palestinians would build their state on 94 per cent of the occupied territories. In return for Israel annexing 6 per cent of occupied land—that is, the major West Bank Israeli settlements—the new state of Palestine would be given the equivalent of 3 per cent in land contiguous to the Gaza Strip. That is, Palestinians would be compensated by a 'land swap', using the 1949 armistice lines as the basis for the border. On the issue of Jerusalem, sovereignty would be shared, with Arab neighbourhoods becoming part of the Palestinian state and Jewish areas, including the Jewish quarter of the Old City, coming under Israeli sovereignty. On the highly sensitive issue of the 'right of return' for Palestinian refugees, Clinton's plan envisaged it being met by their return to the new state of Palestine, not to their original homes which were now part of Israel. In an effort to provide the Clinton parameters with a more detailed framework, Israelis and Palestinians held marathon meetings in the Egyptian resort town of Taba. They concluded the Taba meetings in January 2001 with the announcement that they had never been so close to a resolution of the outstanding issues.

The al-Aqsa *intifada*

The window of opportunity had, however, closed. As one negotiator lamented, 'If Camp David was too little, Taba was too late.' The spirit of compromise had been profoundly overtaken by a second *intifada*, the violent Palestinian uprising that consumed the region for the next few years. Its outbreak resulted from the widespread disillusionment of Palestinians, especially the younger generation, both with the failure of the Oslo peace process to end the daily humiliations of an occupation that had gone on for over thirty years and with the inept and authoritarian rule of Arafat's Palestinian Authority. The pent-up anger exploded in late September 2000, triggered by the provocative visit by Ariel Sharon (successor to Netanyahu as leader of the Likud opposition) to al-Haram al-Sharif (the Noble Sanctuary), the site in East Jerusalem on which stands the golden Dome of the Rock and the al-Aqsa mosque (see Illustration 13). Accompanied by hundreds of Israeli police, Sharon sought to assert that any Jew had the right to visit the site (known to Jews as the Temple Mount), also the location of the Jewish First and Second Temples. Palestinians reacted the following day with stone-throwing demonstrations which were put down by Israeli security forces with lethal force. The death of eighteen protesters at the hands of the Israeli security forces brought to the surface the stresses and strains felt by Palestinians. The demonstrations quickly transformed into a sustained popular uprising that came to be known as the al-Aqsa *intifada* in reference to both the 1987 uprising and to the tensions, in the wake of the Camp David failure, over the question of sovereignty over Jerusalem's holy places. By summer of 2003, some 2,400 Palestinians and 800 Israelis had lost their lives, with thousands more wounded.

13. **Temple Mount/al-Haram al-Sharif (present day)**

As was the case with the first *intifada*, the sudden outbreak of violence took the Palestinian leadership by surprise. But in the volatile environment, marked by widespread mistrust and anger, Arafat did little to restrain the mounting violence. Without a coordinated leadership, the array of militant acts broadened, with Palestinian security forces employing their light automatic weapons and Hamas directing suicide bombing campaigns that targeted Israeli civilians. Pent-up anger also lay behind the intensity of the Israeli response to the uprising. As the cycle of violence gathered steam, the political equations on the ground changed dramatically. Among Palestinians, power became more fragmented: internal discord within Fatah intensified, while Hamas was able to capitalize on its rejection of the failed Oslo process to put forth an increasingly credible challenge to Fatah's position in the Palestinian Authority. In Israel, on the other hand, the suicide attacks in the wake of the Camp David failure traumatized the political left and helped Ariel Sharon defeat Barak in the 2001 elections. In this way, the second *intifada* in effect strengthened the forces of Greater Israel, that is a Jewish state in the region between the Mediterranean and the Jordan River.

Upon coming to power, Sharon set about destroying the Palestinian Authority's political and economic infrastructure. The deployment of helicopters and fighter jets, and the incursions of Israeli Defence Force tanks into Palestinian civilian areas, brought about tremendous human suffering. In the eyes of Israelis, such massive military force was warranted by the overriding concern for security. Israel argued that not only had Arafat consistently failed to comply with the security provisions set out in the Oslo accords, he was now engaging in violence as a strategic gambit to pursue political objectives. Held responsible in these ways, Arafat was confined in 2002 to his office compound in Ramallah, just north of Jerusalem. As the Israeli military forcibly reoccupied Palestinian areas, it effectively undid the Palestinian Authority in all but name, and increased the checkpoints that severely restricted the Palestinians' movements in the occupied territories.

Sharon's actions were bolstered internationally by the events of 9/11, when Islamist militants from Saudi Arabia and Egypt turned airplanes into missiles destroying New York's World Trade Center and part of the Pentagon in Washington DC on 11 September 2001, leaving more than 3,200 people dead. Following these attacks by al-Qaeda, President George W. Bush launched his 'war on terrorism' in which he judged countries either 'with us or against us'. Although some members of the US administration, such as Secretary of State Colin Powell, stressed the need for greater engagement with the Israeli–Palestinian peace process to strengthen the United States in its battle against al-Qaeda, most members of the Bush administration simply regarded Sharon as confronting his own bin Laden in Arafat, and concluded that Israel should be left alone to deal with the terrorist networks threatening it.

Rather than negotiate, Sharon at this stage initiated a unilateral approach towards separating Israelis from Palestinians. The policy came to be known as 'disengagement'. One key component of the policy was the construction of a physical barrier made up of a complex network of barbed write, electric fences, patrol roads, and concrete walls 8 metres (about 26 feet) high. The idea was justified by the need to prevent entry into Israel by suicide bombers. But Palestinians condemned the way the barrier snaked its way well beyond the 1967 border to envelop large Jewish settlement blocs (see Illustration 14). Palestinians claimed that such annexation of land was a violation of international law, a claim upheld by the International Court of Justice in 2004. A second feature of Sharon's disengagement plan involved the removal of 8,000 Jewish settlers from the Gaza Strip, home to 1.3 million Palestinian Arabs. Though he had once personified the settlement ethos, Sharon was increasingly worried about the need to reconcile the dream of a Greater Israel with demographic projections of an approaching Arab majority. Furthermore, the pulling of settlements out of Gaza provided cover for deepening Israeli control over West Bank settlements. As an adviser to Sharon put it, the Gaza withdrawal applied the necessary formaldehyde to freeze the political process.

From the start, Sharon's unilateral disengagement plan was presented as an alternative to negotiation. Arafat was blamed for the violence and rejected as a possible partner in peace. Some observers worried about the impact of isolating and marginalizing Arafat as an enemy of peace: they argued that only 'Mr Palestine' had the mandate for making the painful compromises expected from the Palestinians in a peace settlement. No doubt, the authority of the Palestinian leadership suffered greatly from Arafat's marginalization and the deepening of internal splits within Fatah.

Arafat died of a mysterious illness in 2004. He was succeeded as president of the Palestinian Authority by Mahmoud Abbas (also known as Abu Mazen). Abbas had strongly opposed the second *intifada*, describing it as disastrous for Palestinians. One of the

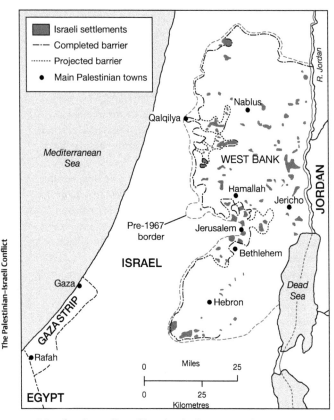

14. Map showing walls and barriers in the West Bank

key architects of the Oslo accords, Abbas remained a believer in
negotiations throughout the escalating cycle of violence. But his
failure to persuade Israel to ease life in the occupied territories
made it extremely difficult for him to rebuild the credibility of
Fatah and to shore up a basis of popular support for continuing
with the Oslo process. In contrast to the fragmentation and
disarray of Fatah, Hamas's power and influence were growing.

With the goal of integrating, and subordinating, Hamas within the constitutional structures created by the Oslo accords, Abbas offered a round of parliamentary elections, set for January 2006. The result stunned everyone. Whereas Fatah had little to show for its diplomatic efforts over a decade, during which Israel's arbitrary restrictions in the occupied territories had in fact increased, Hamas effectively positioned itself during the election campaign to take credit for the evacuation of Israeli settlers from Gaza. Hamas also benefited greatly from the disarray in which Arafat's authoritarian leadership had left Fatah. Despite having dominated the Palestinian legislature for its first decade, Fatah was trounced by Hamas in free and open democratic elections.

Hamas's victory severely complicated Abbas's efforts to restart negotiations with Israel. Both Fatah and much of the international community called for a boycott of the Islamist government until it honoured previous Palestinian commitments that recognized Israel and renounced violence. Fatah officials, meanwhile, continued to behave as though they were still in charge. Political activists from both sides confronted each other in increasingly violent clashes. This was especially the case in Gaza, where deteriorating economic conditions were exacerbated by growing lawlessness. In June 2007, fearing a US-supported effort by Fatah to overthrow it, Hamas brutally but swiftly seized all Fatah bases in the Gaza Strip, and gradually established its own effective control over the territory. Abbas accused Hamas of staging a coup, dismissed the Hamas-led government, and created an emergency cabinet to rule the West Bank separately. With Palestinian society politically as well as geographically divided and Israelis increasingly sceptical of a peaceful settlement, the two-states solution proved more elusive than ever.

Conclusion

The Oslo peace process began, amidst great fanfare and optimism, with the signing of the first Israeli–Palestinian agreement on the

White House Lawn on 13 September 1993. However, from the outset there was fierce opposition on both sides to a diplomatic settlement. The position of the opponents was strengthened by the slow and hesitant progress in implementing the accords. Rather than lead to a final peace treaty, the Oslo Accords contributed instead to greater insecurity for Israelis and, in the occupied Palestinian territories, a more deeply felt, and resented, matrix of Israeli military control.

Although the Oslo accords did eventually lead to a blueprint for a two-states solution, as agreed upon in 2001 at the Egyptian resort town of Taba, the mounting frustration and rising anger on both sides made that plan impossible to implement. The Taba framework promised a resolution to the conflict, but the Oslo process had over eight years gravely deepened the mistrust felt by everyone. Each side accused the other of sabotaging the peace process. Palestinians accused Israel of taking advantage of negotiations to further entrench Jewish settlements on the land they sought for their own state, while Israel accused the Palestinians of equivocating on their commitment to end armed attacks.

In late 2000, the region descended again into a spiral of violence, known as the al-Aqsa *intifada*. Hamas's popularity grew dramatically as political opposition to Fatah rose, and Israelis became increasingly opposed to the idea of living beside an independent Palestinian state. Meanwhile, Jewish settlements in the occupied territories continued to expand, raising real concerns about whether the land of historic Palestine could in fact practically be partitioned.

As a result, the Oslo process ended, on the one hand, with individual negotiators successfully outlining the main ingredients of a peace settlement but, on the other, with the chances of implementing that resolution crushed by the spiralling violence that erupted out of the pent-up mistrust and anger revealed or manufactured over the previous eight years. Like the story of the lost traveller who, after asking for directions to his destination, is told: 'If I were going there, I wouldn't start from here,' no common ground could be found after Taba from which the two sides could begin again down the road to a genuine reconciliation and negotiated peace. The Oslo accords had been premised on the idea that time was needed to build the political space in which negotiations could succeed. Far from healing wounds, the Oslo process rubbed more salt into them.

Conclusion

This is just really hard...This is as intractable a problem as you get.
President Barack Obama, *Time Magazine*
interview, 15 January 2010

First laid out in the Taba accords of early 2001, the parameters
for a resolution of the century-old Palestinian–Israeli conflict have
since been elaborated upon by several initiatives. Each, in turn,
has strengthened the regional and international consensus
supporting a two-states solution. In early 2002, Saudi Arabia
proposed a peace plan that came to be known as the Arab
Peace Initiative when it received the unanimous approval of the
Arab League meeting in Beirut: it promised Israel that in return
for the full withdrawal from all occupied territory Israel would
receive regional recognition and that its relations with the Arab
world would be normalized. In April 2003, the Quartet group
(United States, Europe, Russia, and the United Nations)
announced a three-stage plan known as the 'Road Map' for
bringing an end to the 1967 occupation and the establishment of
an independent Palestine state. In December 2003, prominent
Israeli and Palestinian politicians, many of whom had
participated in the Camp David summit, avoided the usual
recourse to gradual measures and arrived at a comprehensive
agreement: known as the Geneva Initiative, it filled many of the

gaps left by the Taba accords. In 2004, the International Court of Justice called for an end to the construction of the wall which it described as contrary to international law. In June 2009, in a widely anticipated speech delivered in Cairo, Egypt, President Barack Obama underlined the United States' endorsement of a two-states solution:

> For decades...there has been a stalemate: two peoples with legitimate aspirations, each with a painful history that makes compromise elusive. It's easy to point fingers—for Palestinians to point to the displacement brought about by Israel's founding, and for Israelis to point to the constant hostility and attacks throughout its history from within its borders as well as beyond. But if we see this conflict only from one side or the other, then we will be blind to the truth: The only resolution is for the aspirations of both sides to be met through two states, where Israelis and Palestinians each live in peace and security.
>
> That is in Israel's interest, Palestine's interest, America's interest, and the world's interest.

Finally, on 29 November 2012—sixty-five years after the two-states solution first garnered explicit international recognition—the United Nations General Assembly recognized a Palestinian state.

Text of the United Nations General Assembly resolution on the status of Palestine

29 November 2012

The General Assembly,

Guided by the purposes and principles of the Charter of the United Nations, and stressing in this regard the principle of equal rights and self-determination of peoples...

Stressing the importance of maintaining and strengthening international peace founded upon freedom, equality, justice and respect for fundamental human rights,

Recalling its resolution 181 (II) of 29 November 1947 ...

Reaffirming also relevant Security Council resolutions, including, inter alia, resolutions 242 (1967) of 22 November 1967, 338 (1973) of 22 October 1973 ...

Recalling the advisory opinion of the International Court of Justice of 9 July 2004 ...

Recalling also the Arab Peace Initiative adopted in March 2002 by the Council of the League of Arab States,

Reaffirming its commitment, in accordance with international law, to the two-State solution of an independent, sovereign, democratic, viable and contiguous State of Palestine living side by side with Israel in peace and security on the basis of the pre-1967 borders ...

1. *Reaffirms* the right of the Palestinian people to self-determination and to independence in their State of Palestine on the Palestinian territory occupied since 1967;

2. *Decides* to accord to Palestine non-member observer State status in the United Nations, without prejudice to the acquired rights, privileges and role of the Palestine Liberation Organization in the United Nations as the representative of the Palestinian people, in accordance with the relevant resolutions and practice;

3. *Expresses the hope* that the Security Council will consider favourably the application submitted on 23 September 2011 by the State of Palestine for admission to full membership in the United Nations;

4. *Affirms* its determination to contribute to the achievement of the inalienable rights of the Palestinian people and the

attainment of a peaceful settlement in the Middle East that ends the occupation that began in 1967 and fulfils the vision of two States: an independent, sovereign, democratic, contiguous and viable State of Palestine living side by side in peace and security with Israel on the basis of the pre-1967 borders;

5. *Expresses the urgent need* for the resumption and acceleration of negotiations within the Middle East peace process based on the relevant United Nations resolutions, the terms of reference of the Madrid Conference, including the principle of land for peace, the Arab Peace Initiative and the Quartet road map to a permanent two-State solution to the Israeli–Palestinian conflict for the achievement of a just, lasting and comprehensive peace settlement between the Palestinian and Israeli sides that resolves all outstanding core issues, namely the Palestine refugees, Jerusalem, settlements, borders, security and water;

6. *Urges* all States, the specialized agencies and organizations of the United Nations system to continue to support and assist the Palestinian people in the early realization of their right to self-determination, independence and freedom;

7. *Requests* the Secretary-General to take the necessary measures to implement the present resolution and to report to the Assembly within three months on progress made in this regard.

44th plenary meeting

29 November 2012

The basic outlines for the resolution of the Palestinian–Israeli conflict are clear. First, the emergence of two states with clear boundaries based on the 1949 armistice lines (sometimes referred to as the Green Line or the pre-June 1967 border): minor and reciprocal territorial exchanges would leave some heavily populated Jewish settlements located close to the Green Line in situ without compromising the contiguity and viability of the Palestinian state. Second, the sharing of Jerusalem as the capital of both Israel and Palestine: Israel would retain sovereignty over many Jewish settlements close to the Green Line, Palestinians would gain sovereignty over Arab neighbourhoods, and a shared regime would provide both sides with unimpeded access to the respective holy places. Third, a mutually acceptable negotiation of the Palestinian refugee problem: morally a resolution would require acknowledgement of the unjust displacement brought about by Israel's founding, while practically it would be based on meaningful financial compensation and a 'return' to the new state of Palestine, without ruling out a return to homes in Israel so long as the Jewish character of the state was not threatened. Fourth, limitations placed on the Palestinian military forces established to provide security in the new Palestinian state.

All this means that the parameters of a two-state solution are well known and well rehearsed. And yet the prospects for a two-states solution are in fact fading, undermined by hardliners on both sides who refuse to accept the establishment of two states within the borders of mandate Palestine and by rapidly changing facts on the ground.

On the Palestinian side, efforts towards a two-states solution have been paralysed by the absence of a unified leadership and coherent strategy. To be sure, long-term centrifugal forces have fragmented Palestinian society into pieces (West Bank, East Jerusalem, Gaza, and the refugees' host countries). Most recently, the intra-Palestinian violence in 2007 culminated in the political separation of Fatah in the West Bank and its bitter rival Hamas in the Gaza Strip. An effective Palestinian national strategy for self-determination requires, above all, reconciliation between the nationalist Fatah party, which signed on to bilateral negotiations under international sponsorship, and the Islamist Hamas party, which believes in achieving this goal through confrontation and resistance. Though the United States and Israel have pushed to exclude Hamas, which they consider a terrorist organization, Palestinian unity is essential to the peace process: were a weakened Fatah to reach an agreement with Israel on a two-states solution, it is not clear that it alone has the legitimacy or credibility to sign off on it. Any agreement that a large majority of Palestinians did not accept would play into the hands of Hamas and make such a state tougher to govern effectively. It would not bring about a lasting peace.

But a unified platform will require subjecting the armed irredentism of Hamas to greater scrutiny, and concluding a genuine ceasefire agreement with Israel. In order for Israelis to conceive of a neighbouring Palestinian state being in their interests, the question of security is paramount. Although Hamas has never offered permanent recognition of Israel, various leaders have pledged acceptance of a long-term truce or *hudna* in exchange for a two-states solution. Hamas leaders have also said that the party would accept, if not endorse the establishment of a Palestinian state within the 1967 borders provided that the compromise was approved by a majority of Palestinians in a referendum.

Many Palestinians are evidently frustrated with both Fatah and Hamas for perpetuating what is viewed as a self-serving division. But reconciling the schism between the two parties, which are themselves internally divided, has been a real challenge given the ongoing diplomatic stalemate. The deepening occupation tends to bolster the legitimacy of Hamas: its military clashes with Israel allow it to be portrayed as heroic in its resistance. Meanwhile Fatah faces increased marginalization, as it struggles to avoid the charge that the Palestinian Authority it heads is little more than a fig leaf for an expanding Israeli occupation.

On the Israeli side, negotiations towards a two-states solution are paralysed chiefly by the challenge of containing, let alone reversing, settlement construction. The settler population has reached over 500,000, and it is growing at a faster rate than the rest of the Israeli population. To be sure, those settlers who see Jewish sovereignty over all of the territory of mandate Palestine—'Greater Israel'—as a Biblical right, as well as a national obligation, are a minority. Nonetheless they are a powerful constituency and, considering how Israel's system of proportional government allows small parties to make strident demands, they present dangerous political risks to any government that seeks to remove them. One need only consider, for example, the challenge presented by the old city of Hebron where holy sites such as the Tomb of the Patriarchs (Abraham, Isaac, and Jacob)—a building shared with the Ibrahimi mosque—have been tightly integrated into the settlement infrastructure.

In 2009 Israeli voters elected Benjamin Netanyahu as prime minister for the second time. Later that year, he endorsed the two-states solution in a speech delivered at Bar Ilan University in which he envisaged a future where 'two peoples live freely, side by side, in amity and mutual respect'. But no plan to bring a state into being was produced, and his vision has in fact been repudiated by the actions taken since then, in particular the significant expansion of settlement construction in East Jerusalem.

Although the Likud-led government under Netanyahu appeared confident that the stalemated status quo could continue indefinitely, some observers felt that such complacency is dangerous. The years 2011 and 2012 witnessed transformational events that suggest the unravelling of an old order across the Arab world, and carry the potential to regionalize and internationalize the conflict. On the one hand, the Arab uprisings that brought down authoritarian regimes in Tunisia, Egypt, Yemen, and Libya have drawn closer attention to the Palestinians' desire for democracy and dignity. The cost to Israel of its occupation of Palestinian land would rise significantly if challenged by an outbreak of another Palestinian uprising. A non-violent mass mobilization, modelled on the popular mobilization of the 1987 *intifada*, may convince the Israeli government that the vision of a sustainable or comfortable status quo is an illusion. It might also force the United States to make a serious push to bring about a two-states solution. Meanwhile, the November 2012 United Nations resolution that raised the status of Palestine to that of a non-member observer state also carries the potential to shake up the status quo. The resolution reaffirms Israel's right to peace and security within its pre-1967 borders, but also clearly undermines the legitimacy of Israeli settlements that lie beyond those borders. Furthermore, Palestine's upgraded status may allow it recourse to the International Criminal Court in the Hague.

Although it appears to be steadily eroding, there does remain broad public support amongst both Israelis and Palestinians for the prescription of a two-states solution to this century-long conflict. What are lacking are the political will and capacity of Israeli and Palestinian leaders to implement the solution. As long as the leaders are left to fix it themselves, the chances of a diplomatic breakthrough appear low. But in the absence of an urgent shift out of the current diplomatic impasse, the prevailing one-state framework will be further consolidated. Indeed, some observers suspect that Israel's settlement programme in the West Bank will soon render impossible a two-states solution.

The expansion of settlements in the decade since the Taba accords has raised grave doubts about whether the land between the Mediterranean Sea and the Jordan River can in fact be partitioned into two viable states. Of particular concern is the extent to which the deepening of settlement infrastructure (housing as well as fenced-off access roads) has eaten into the West Bank, blocking the establishment of a viable and contiguous Palestinian state. The core of the West Bank highway infrastructure, for example, now belongs to the Israeli settlements. Moreover, the continued encirclement of East

Jerusalem by a ring of Jewish settlements not only isolates it from the rest of the West Bank but also effectively bisects the region into northern and southern parts.

In the absence of a two-states solution, Israel will face two options. One scenario posits a shared homeland: a binational state with equal rights for the two national communities that evolved from it. Israelis in their homes on the coastal plain would be free to walk the hills of ancient Judea and Samaria while Palestinians who can see the Mediterranean Sea from their hill villages would be able to swim in it. This scenario would cost Israel its dream of a Jewish state. The alternative costs Israel its democracy. The second scenario concludes that Jewish history has been too traumatic for Israelis to accept being a minority but recognizes that the Palestinian Arab population is growing more rapidly than the Jewish Israeli population. Such a situation can only end up consigning Palestinians to autonomous and fragmented Bantustans. In 2007, former Israeli Prime Minister Ehud Olmert indeed warned that the coming demographic parity of Arabs and Jews in the land of historic Palestine would necessarily carry the danger of forcing Israel to become an apartheid-like state. In 2010, former Prime Minister Ehud Barak echoed the diagnosis: 'If, and as long as between the Jordan and the sea, there is only one political entity, named Israel, it will end up being either non-Jewish or nondemocratic . . . If the Palestinians vote in elections, it is a binational state, and if they don't, it is an apartheid state.'

Chronology

1858, 1867: Ottoman government passes new land laws during era of *Tanzimat* reforms.

1869: Suez Canal opens.

1896: Theodor Herzl's *Der Judenstaat* published.

1897: Founding of World Zionist Organization at Basel, Switzerland.

1901: Establishment of Jewish National Fund for purchasing land in Palestine.

1904-14: Second *aliyah*, or wave of Jewish immigration, to Palestine.

1914: Ottoman Empire joins war as ally to Germany.

1915-16: Husayn–McMahon correspondence promises an Arab kingdom to Sharif Husyan of the Hijaz.

1916: Sykes–Picot Agreement divides up the Arab Middle East between Britain and France.

1917: Balfour Declaration supports 'the establishment in Palestine of a national home for the Jewish people', though without prejudicing its non-Jewish communities. British troops enter Jerusalem.

1918: Woodrow Wilson proclaims Fourteen Points.

1920: At the San Remo Conference, following their victory over the Ottoman Empire, Allied powers approve British administration of Palestine, Transjordan, and Iraq. First large-scale clashes between Zionists and Arabs in Palestine.

1923: Britain's mandate over Palestine officially ratified by the League of Nations. British fail to set up an elected legislative council.

1929: Western (Wailing) Wall riots.

1930: Britain issues Passfield White Paper, calling for restrictions on Jewish immigration and land purchase and drawing attention to the continued absence of legislative council.

1931: MacDonald letter, in which British Prime Minister revokes key elements of 1930 White Paper.

1936: Palestinian Arab demonstrations spontaneously erupt amid frustration at continued colonial rule and rising Jewish immigration. Britain dispatches Peel Commission to investigate underlying causes.

1937: Peel Commission recommends partition. Second stage of Arab revolt begins.

1939: Britain issues White Paper, imposing restrictions on Jewish immigration and land purchase and calling for an independent Palestine state.

1942: Biltmore conference held in New York City, calling for a Jewish state over all of Palestine.

1945: At end of the Second World War, United States pressures Britain to relax its restrictions on Jewish refugees settling in Palestine.

1946: Jewish militant group, Irgun, blows up King David Hotel, Britain's headquarters in Jerusalem.

1947: Britain asks United Nations (UN) to take over Palestine mandate. United Nations Special Committee on Palestine (UNSCOP) recommends partition. The Arabs reject it, but UN General Assembly approves (Resolution 181). Civil war breaks out in Palestine.

1948: State of Israel proclaimed. Units of Arab armies invade. Over 700,000 Palestinian Arabs are expelled or flee the fighting. Israel declares independence on more land (including West Jerusalem) than originally proposed by UN. Egypt occupies Gaza Strip and Transjordan annexes East Jerusalem and the West Bank.

1956:	Egyptian President Gamal Abd al-Nasser nationalizes the Suez Canal Company. Israel, France, and Britain work to topple Nasser and invade Egypt. United States pressures them to withdraw.
1964:	The Palestine Liberation Organization (PLO) created under auspices of Arab League.
1967:	Israel decisively defeats Egypt, Syria, and Jordan in span of six days. Sinai Peninsula and Gaza Strip are taken from Egypt; West Bank (including East Jerusalem) from Jordan; and Golan Heights from Syria. The UN Security Council approves Resolution 242, calling for an exchange of land for peace. Arab countries meeting at Khartoum issue their 'three noes': no recognition, no negotiation, and no peace with Israel.
1969:	Yasir Arafat elected head of PLO. Egypt launches 'war of attrition' against Israel.
1970:	Jordan's King Husayn expels the PLO, which re-establishes itself in Lebanon.
1973:	Surprise attack in October by Egypt and Syria on Israel. 'Shuttle diplomacy' by US Secretary of State and National Security Adviser Henry Kissinger aims at a political settlement.
1974:	Gush Emunim (Bloc of the Faithful) formed to create Jewish settlements in the occupied territories.
1975:	Civil war breaks out in Lebanon.
1977:	Menachem Begin elected Prime Minister of Israel. Egypt's President Anwar Sadat visits Israel.
1978:	Talks at Camp David end in peace accord between Israel and Egypt.
1979:	Israel and Egypt sign peace treaty in which Israel returns the occupied Sinai Peninsula to Egypt.
1982:	Israel invades Lebanon. The PLO is exiled to Tunisia. Palestinians in the Sabra and Shatila refugee camps are massacred by Lebanese Christian militia allied to Israel.
1987:	Palestinians launch the first *intifada* ('shaking-off') against Israeli occupation of the West Bank and Gaza

Strip. Hamas founded as an offshoot of the Muslim Brotherhood.

1988: Jordan drops its claim to sovereignty over the West Bank. PLO affirms UN Resolution 242, renounces terrorism, and recognizes Israel.

1991: After Gulf War ends, the United States convenes an international peace conference in Madrid, in which all states of the region participated (though not the PLO).

1993: Secret talks in Oslo between Israeli academics and PLO officials lead to the Oslo accords.

1994: PLO chairman Arafat returns to the occupied territories to head the Palestinian Authority. Israel signs a peace treaty with Jordan.

1995: Israel and PLO sign Oslo II agreement, dividing the West Bank into three zones and calling for further Israeli withdrawals. Israeli Prime Minister Yitzhak Rabin assassinated during peace rally in Tel Aviv.

1998: At the Wye Summit, Israeli Prime Minister Benjamin Netanyahu and Arafat set a timetable for implementation of Oslo II agreement.

1999: After more slippage in Oslo process, Israeli Prime Minister Ehud Barak and Arafat set another timetable for implementation of Oslo agreements.

2000: Camp David summit, hosted by US president Bill Clinton, ends in failure. Israel's opposition leader, Ariel Sharon, visits Jerusalem's Temple Mount/al-Haram al-Sharif. Palestinians launch second *intifada*.

2001: Israeli and Palestinian delegations hold talks at Taba in Egypt. Al-Qaeda terrorists attack World Trade Center and Pentagon.

2002: Israel launches Operation Defensive Shield, controlling areas of the Palestinian Authority, and begins construction of separation barrier. Saudi Arabia's peace initiative receives unanimous approval at the Arab League meeting in Beirut.

2003: The Quartet group (America, the European Union, Russia, and the UN) issues the 'Road Map', a three-stage plan for creating an independent Palestine. Prominent Israeli and Palestinian politicians, many of whom had participated in the Camp David summit, launch the Geneva Initiative, aimed at a comprehensive agreement.

2004: The International Court of Justice calls for an end to the illegal situation resulting from the wall and its associated regime. Arafat dies in a Paris hospital and Mahmoud Abbas succeeds him as president of the Palestinian Authority.

2005: Israeli Prime Minister Ariel Sharon evacuates all settlements in the Gaza Strip.

2006: Hamas wins Palestinian parliamentary elections.

2007: Hamas seizes Fatah bases in Gaza Strip, taking full control of the area.

2009: In a speech at Bar Ilan university, Israeli Prime Minister Benjamin Netanyahu for the first time endorses the establishment of a Palestinian state.

2011: Mass Arab uprisings topple dictatorships in Tunisia, Egypt, Yemen, and Libya.

2012: UN General Assembly Resolution upgrades Palestine's status at the UN to 'non-member state'.

References

Preface

David Ben Gurion quoted in Avi Shlaim, *The Iron Wall: Israel and the Arab World* (New York: W. W. Norton, 2000).

Shibley Telhami, *The Stakes: America and the Middle East: The Consequences of Power and the Choice for Peace* (Boulder: Westview Press, 2002).

Chapter 1: Ottoman Palestine 1897–1917

Ahad Ha'am quoted in Benny Morris, *Righteous Victims: A History of the Zionist-Arab Conflict, 1881–2001* (New York: Vintage Books, 2001), pp. 42–9.

Menachem Ussishkin quoted in Gershon Shafir, *Land, Labor and the Origins of the Israeli-Palestinian Conflict, 1882–1914*, updated edition (Berkeley: University of California Press, 1996), p. 42.

Golda Meir quoted in James Gelvin, *The Israel–Palestine Conflict: One Hundred Years of War* (Cambridge: Cambridge University Press, 2007), p. 92.

E. C. Willatts, 'Some Geographical Factors in the Palestine Problem' *The Geographical Journal*, 108/4 (1946), pp. 146–73.

Newt Gingrich quoted in 'Palestinians are an Invented People, says Newt Gingrich', *The Guardian*, 10 December 2011, http://www.guardian.co.uk/world/2011/dec/10/palestinians-invented-people-newt-gingrich

Theodor Herzl quoted in David W. Lesch, *The Arab–Israeli Conflict: A History* (New York: Oxford University Press, 2008), p. 32.

Chapter 2: British Palestine 1917–37

George Antonius and Sir Henry McMahon quoted in Jonathan Schneer, *The Balfour Declaration: The Origins of the Arab–Israeli Conflict* (New York: Random House, 2010), pp. 69 and 85.

Lord Balfour quoted in Tom Segev, *One Palestine, Complete: Jews and Arabs under the British Mandate* (New York: Henry Holt and Company, 2000), p. 45.

Mayir Vereté, 'The Balfour Declaration and its Makers', *Middle Eastern Studies*, 6 (1970), p. 50.

D. K. Fieldhouse, *Western Imperialism in the Middle East, 1914–1958* (Oxford, New York: Oxford University Press, 2006), p. 155.

Elizabeth Monroe quoted in Avi Shlaim, *Israel and Palestine: Reappraisals, Revisions, Refutations* (London: Verso, 2010), p. 4.

Lord Curzon quoted in James Renton, *The Zionist Masquerade: The Birth of the Anglo–Zionist Alliance 1914–1918* (Basingstoke: Palgrave Macmillan, 2007), p. 72.

Chapter 3: Palestine partitioned 1937–47

Palestine Royal Commission Report (Peel Report), Cmd. 5479 (July 1937).

Chaim Weizmann quoted in Christopher Sykes, *Crossroads to Israel, 1917–1948* (Bloomington: Indiana University Press, 1973).

David Ben Gurion quoted in Avi Shlaim, *The Iron Wall: Israel and the Arab World* (New York: W. W. Norton, 2000).

Ivan Rand and George Kirk quoted in Wm Roger Louis, *The British Empire in the Middle East, 1945–1951: Arab Nationalism, the United States and Postwar Imperialism* (Oxford, New York: Oxford University Press, 1984), p. 471.

Richard M. Graves, *Experiment in Anarchy* (London: Victor Gollancz, 1949), p. 132.

Edward Mortimer, 'It's Better Late...Palestinian rejectionism was usually justified, but always wrong', *The Financial Times*, 15 September 1993, p. 24.

Chapter 4: *Atzmaut* and *Nakba* 1947–67

Plan D quoted in Benny Morris, *1948: A History of the First Arab–Israeli War* (New Haven: Yale University Press, 2008), pp. 120–1.

Avi Shlaim, 'Israel and the Arab Coalition in 1948', in *The War for Palestine*, edited by Eugene L. Rogan and Avi Shlaim (Cambridge: Cambridge University Press, 2001), p. 100.

Michael Fischbach, *Jewish Property Claims against Arab Countries* (New York: Columbia University Press, 2008).

Tom Segev, *1967: Israel, the War, and the Year that Transformed the Middle East,* trans. Jessica Cohen (New York: Metropolitan Books, 2007).

Roger Owen, *State, Power and Politics in the Making of the Modern Middle East* (London, New York: Routledge, 2004), pp. 60–2.

Chapter 5: Occupation 1967–87

William Quandt, *Peace Process: American Diplomacy and the Arab–Israel Conflict since 1967* (Berkeley: University of California Press, 1993).

Ian Lustick, *For the Land and the Lord: Jewish Fundamentalism in Israel* (New York: Council on Foreign Relations, 1988).

Bernard Wasserstein, *Divided Jerusalem: The Struggle for the Holy City* (New Haven and London: Yale University Press, 2001).

Helena Cobban, *The Palestinian Liberation Organisation: People, Power and Politics* (Cambridge: Cambridge University Press, 1984).

Yezid Sayigh, *Armed Struggle and the Search for State: The Palestinian National Movement, 1949–1993* (Oxford: Oxford University Press, 1997).

Chapter 6: The rise and fall of the peace process 1987–2007

F. Robert Hunter, *The Palestinian Uprising: A War by Other Means* (Berkeley: University of California Press, 1993).

Glenn E. Robinson, *Building a Palestinian State: The Incomplete Revolution* (Bloomington: Indiana University Press, 1997).

Rabin and Arafat quoted in Tom Friedman, 'Rabin and Arafat Seal Their Accord as Clinton Applauds "Brave Gamble"', *New York Times*, 13 September 1993, p. 1.

Robert Malley and Hussein Agha, 'Camp David: The Tragedy of Errors,' *New York Review of Books*, 48/13 (August, 2001), 59–65.

Deborah Sontag, 'And Yet so Far: A Special Report; Quest for Mideast Peace: How and Why it Failed', *New York Times*, 26 July 2001.

Sharm El-Sheikh Fact-Finding Committee Final Report (The Mitchell Report), 30 April 2001, http://2001-2009.state.gov/p/nea/rls/rpt/3060.htm

Conclusion

'Cairo speech' by President Barack Obama and 'Bar Ilan Speech' by Prime Minster Benjamin Netanyahu can be found in *The Contemporary Middle East: A Westview Reader*, edited by Karl Yambert (Boulder: Westview, 2010).

Mouin Rabbani, 'A Hamas Perspective on the Movement's Evolving Role: An Interview with Khalid Mishal: Part II', in *Journal of Palestine Studies*, 37/4 (Summer 2008), 59–81.

Nathan Brown, 'The Palestinians' Receding Dream of Statehood', in *Current History*, 110 (December 2011), 345–51.

Prime Minister Ehud Olmert quoted in Aluf Benn, David Landau, Barak Ravid, and Shmuel Rosner, 'Olmert to Haaretz: Two-State Solution, or Israel is Done For', *Haaretz*, 29 November 2007.

Prime Minister Ehud Barak quoted in 'Barak Breaks the Apartheid Barrier', *The Economist*, 15 February 2010, http://www.economist.com/blogs/democracyinamerica/2010/02/israel_demography_democracy_or_apartheid

Further reading

General texts

Caplan, Neil. *The Israel–Palestine Conflict: Contested Histories* (Chichester: Wiley-Blackwell, 2010).

Cleveland, William L. *A History of the Modern Middle East* (Boulder: Westview Press, 2004).

Gelvin, James. *The Israel–Palestine Conflict: One Hundred Years of War* (Cambridge: Cambridge University Press, 2007).

Kimmerling, Baruch and Joel S. Migdal. *The Palestinian People: A History* (Cambridge, MA: Harvard University Press, 2003).

Lesch, Ann M. *Origins and Development of the Arab–Israeli Conflict*, revised edition (Westport: Greenwood Press, 2006).

Lesch, David W. *The Arab–Israeli Conflict: A History* (New York: Oxford University Press, 2008).

Lucas, Noah. *The Modern History of Israel* (London: Weidenfeld and Nicolson, 1974).

Morris, Benny. *Righteous Victims: A History of the Zionist–Arab Conflict, 1881–2001* (New York: Vintage Books, 2001).

Owen, Roger. *State, Power and Politics in the Making of the Modern Middle East* (London, New York: Routledge, 2004).

Pappé, Ilan. *A History of Modern Palestine: One Land, Two Peoples* (Cambridge, New York: Cambridge University Press, 2006).

Rogan, Eugene. *The Arabs: A History* (New York: Basic Books, 2009).

Shlaim, Avi. *The Iron Wall: Israel and the Arab World* (New York: W. W. Norton, 2000).

Smith, Charles D. *Palestine and the Arab–Israeli Conflict: A History with Documents* (Boston, New York: Bedford/St Martin's, 2010).

Yapp, Malcolm. *The Near East since the First World War: A History to 1995*, second edition (Harlow: Longman, 1996).

Chapter 1: Ottaman Palestine 1897–1917

Avineri, Shlomo. *The Making of Modern Zionism: The Intellectual Origins of the Jewish State* (New York: Basic Books, 1981).

Doumani, Beshara. *Rediscovering Palestine: Merchants and Peasants in Jabal Nablus, 1700–1900* (Berkeley: University of California Press, 1995).

Khalidi, Rashid. *Palestinian Identity: The Construction of Modern National Consciousness* (New York: Columbia University Press, 1997).

Owen, Roger. *The Middle East in the World Economy 1800–1914* (London: I.B. Tauris, 1993).

Reilly, James. 'The Peasantry of Late Ottoman Palestine', *Journal of Palestine Studies*, 10/4 (Summer 1981), 82–97.

Vital, David. *The Origins of Zionism* (Oxford: Clarendon Press, 1975).

Chapter 2: British Palestine 1917–37

Khalidi, Rashid. *The Iron Cage: The Story of the Palestinian Struggle for Statehood* (Boston: Beacon Press, 2006).

Lesch, Ann Mosely. *Arab Politics in Palestine, 1917–1939: The Frustration of a National Movement* (Ithaca: Cornell University Press, 1979).

Palestine Royal Commission Report (Peel Report), Cmd. 5479 (July 1937).

Shepherd, Naomi. *Ploughing Sand: British Rule in Palestine, 1917–1948* (New Brunswick: Rutgers University Press, 2000).

Wasserstein, Bernard. *The British in Palestine: The Mandatory Government and the Arab–Jewish Conflict, 1917–1929*, second edition (Oxford: Basil Blackwell, 1979).

Chapter 3: Palestine partitioned 1937–47

Cohen, Michael J. *Palestine and the Great Powers, 1945–1948* (Princeton: Princeton University Press, 1982).

Hitchens, Christopher. 'The Perils of Partition', *Atlantic Monthly*, 291/2 (March 2003), 99–107.

Hurewitz, J. C. *The Struggle for Palestine* (New York: Greenwood Press, 1968).

Louis, Wm Roger and Robert W. Stookey, eds. *The End of the Palestine Mandate* (Austin: University of Texas Press, 1986).

Swedenburg, Ted. *Memories of Revolt: The 1936–1939 Rebellion and the Palestinian National Past* (Minneapolis: University of Minnesota Press, 1995).

Chapter 4: *Atzmaut* and *Nakba* 1947–67

Benvenisti, Meron. *Sacred Landscape: The Buried History of the Holy Land since 1948*, trans. Maxine Kaufman-Lacusta (Berkeley: University of California Press, 2000).

Elon, Amos. *The Israelis: Founders and Sons* (New York: Holt, Rinehart and Winston, 1971).

Kanafani, Ghassan. *Men in the Sun and Other Palestinian Stories*, trans. Hilary Kilpatrick (Boulder: Lynne Rienner, 1999).

Lustick, Ian. *Arabs in the Jewish State: Israel's Control of a National Minority* (Austin: University of Texas Press, 1980).

Rogan, Eugene and Avi Shlaim, eds. *The War for Palestine: Rewriting the History of 1948* (Cambridge: Cambridge University Press, 2007).

Chapter 5: Occupation 1967–87

Horowitz, Dan and Moshe Lissak. *Trouble in Utopia: The Overburdened Polity of Israel* (Albany: State University of New York Press, 1989).

McDowall, David. *The Palestinians* (London: Minority Rights Group International, 1998).

Oz, Amos. *In the Land of Israel* (San Diego: Harcourt Brace, 1993).

Roy, Sara. *The Gaza Strip: The Political Economy of De-development* (Washington: Institute for Palestine Studies, 1995).

Schiff, Ze'ev and Ehud Ya'ari. *Israel's Lebanon War* (New York: Simon and Schuster, 1984).

Chapter 6: The rise and fall of the peace process 1987–2007

Ben-Ami, Shlomo. *Scars of War, Wounds of Peace: The Israel–Arab Tragedy* (Oxford: Oxford University Press, 2007).

Enderlin, Charles. *Shattered Dreams: The Failure of the Peace Process in the Middle East, 1995–2002* (New York: Other Press, 2003).

Hanieh, Akram. 'The Camp David Papers', *Journal of Palestine Studies*, 30/2 (Winter 2001), 75–97.

Hass, Amira. *Drinking the Sea at Gaza: Days and Nights in Land under Seige*, trans. Leana Wesley and Maxine Kaufman-Lacusta (New York: Henry Holt and Company, 1999).

Mishal, Shaul and Avraham Sela. *The Palestinian Hamas: Vision, Violence, and Coexistence* (New York: Columbia University Press, 1996).

Index